Can I Afford Time for Friendships?

Answers to Questions Women Ask About Friends

Answers to Questions Women Ask

Can I Control My Changing Emotions?
Can I Afford Time for Friendships?
Can a Busy Christian Develop Her Spiritual Life?

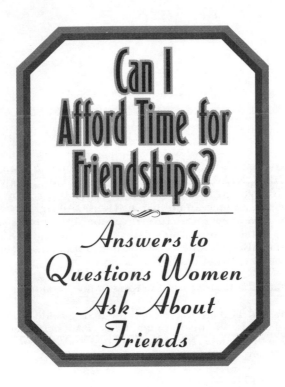

Can I Afford Time for Friendships?

Answers to Questions Women Ask About Friends

Stormie Omartian

Ruth Senter

Colleen Evans

BETHANY HOUSE PUBLISHERS
Minneapolis, Minnesota 55438

All scripture quotations, unless indicated, are taken from the
HOLY BIBLE, NEW INTERNATIONAL VERSION®. Copyright ©
1973, 1978, 1984 by International Bible Society. Used by
permission of Zondervan Publishing House. All rights reserved.
The "NIV" and "New International Version" trademarks are
registered in the United States Patent and Trademark Office by
International Bible Society. Use of either trademark requires the
permission of International Bible Society.

Verses marked KJV are from the King James Version of the Bible.

Verses marked TLB are taken from the Living Bible © 1971 owned
by assignment by Illinois Regional Bank N.A. (as trustee). Used by
permission of Tyndale House Publishers, Inc. Wheaton, IL 60189.
All rights reserved.

Published by Bethany House Publishers
A Ministry of Bethany Fellowship, Inc.
11300 Hampshire Avenue South
Minneapolis, Minnesota 55438

Printed in the United States of America

Library of Congress Cataloging-in-Publication Data

Omartian, Stormie.
    Can I afford time for friendships? / Stormie Omartian, Ruth
Senter, Colleen Evans.
        p.   cm.

    1. Friendship—Religious aspects—Christianity. 2. Women—
Religious life. I. Senter, Ruth Hollinger, 1944–   . II. Evans,
Colleen Townsend. III. Title.
BV4647.F7053   1994
241'.676'082—dc20   94–27810
ISBN 1–55661–517–5   CIP

STORMIE OMARTIAN is the author of four books, including her best-selling autobiography, *Stormie*, and *A Step in the Right Direction: Your Guide to Inner Happiness*. She also has created five popular exercise videos and is a sought-after seminar speaker.

RUTH SENTER is the Senior Editor of *Campus Life* magazine. She is the author of eight books, including *The Seasons of Friendship* and, most recently, *When You're on Your Own*.

COLLEEN EVANS is the author of eight-plus books and has been a minister's wife for more than thirty-five years. She has been involved in inner-city ministries to the poor and is currently spending time in renewal ministries with her husband, Louis Evans, Jr., through the United States and abroad.

Contents

Part Three
Friendship Builders

Epilogue

INTRODUCTION

THE INDISPENSABLE BLESSING

WHEN ASKED BY the editors of a popular women's magazine what is indispensable, Elizabeth Dole, president of the American Red Cross and former Secretary of Labor and Transportation, summed it up in four words, "Faith, family, and friends."

Friends. Where would we be without those special people in our lives who share our joys and sorrows, support and encourage us, understand us, and accept us unconditionally? Friends are indeed a blessing.

And while friendship can be filled with many joys, it can present its share of challenges. Friendship comes at a price. It doesn't just happen—it takes effort and time. Friends don't just appear—they must be sought out. Friendship isn't just one-sided—it takes being a friend to have a friend.

How do we cultivate those friendships we so desire to be part of our lives? How do we develop deep and valued bonds with certain individuals? How do we keep a friendship vital and growing through the years? The answers to these questions often come through trial and error.

While the contributors to this book don't claim to be "friendship experts," each thoughtfully and honestly shares her insights on what she has learned about friendship. It is our hope that their insights will eliminate some of the trial and error in your life as you seek to safely navigate through the sometimes rough relational waters of friendship. In this book you will find in-

sights into the basics of lasting friendships, help to im-
prove the skills necessary to build friendships, and,
finally, ways to break down some of the barriers to satisfying friendships.

The chapters in this book are based on personal interviews conducted in January 1992, and follow-up tele-
phone interviews. Also featured in selected chapters are
excerpts from the pages of *Today's Christian Woman*
magazine, as well as a section titled, "Make It Happen,"
which offers practical ways for you to quickly and easily
implement the specific suggestions made in each chapter.

About the Contributors

Answering the questions in this book are Colleen
Evans, Stormie Omartian, and Ruth Senter, three
women who have weathered the ins and outs of friendship in all different stages and circumstances.

One peek into *Colleen Evans'* home and you'll soon
know that friends hold a top spot in her life. Throughout
her home is photo after photo of those close to her
heart—family, and the many, many friends she has made
over the years. Colleen, in her instantly warm and gracious manner, is someone you instantly *want* to be
friends with.

In between their ministry trips, she and her husband,
Louis, live in the high sierra of California. She has been
a ministry wife for over thirty-five years. Louie, with
Colleen, was founding pastor of the Bel Air Presbyterian
Church in Los Angeles, then they served the La Jolla
Presbyterian Church in La Jolla, California, and the Na-
tional Presbyterian Church in Washington, D.C. Over
the years Colleen has written eight books and has been
personally involved in inner-city ministries to the poor.
She and Louie have reared four children—now grown

and married. They have six grandchildren and are eagerly expecting more!

In the summer of 1991, the Evanses returned to their native California where Louie serves as pastor-at-large for the Menlo Park Presbyterian Church. Together, Louie and Colleen spend half their time in renewal ministries throughout the United States and abroad.

"Be persistent in your friendships," advises Colleen. "If you really value someone as a friend, don't give up on her when the stresses of life are great. There are times when we shouldn't expect certain things from a friend—we should instead just be willing to give."

Many know *Stormie Omartian* as a recognized health and fitness authority. Soft-spoken and deeply sensitive, Stormie admits, "Friendship is extremely important to me—maybe more so than for most people because of my being so alone and without friends in my childhood." In her best-selling autobiography *Stormie* (Harvest House), she recounts the abuse she endured as a child and her eventual healing as an adult through God's help. Stormie's latest book, *A Step in the Right Direction: Your Guide to Inner Happiness* (Thomas Nelson), came as a result of the "deluge" of mail she received from the readers of *Stormie* who wanted practical help with their emotional health. Besides writing, Stormie has created five exercise videos, three with a "gold" status for sales, and is a sought-after seminar speaker. Stormie lives in Nashville, Tennessee, with her husband, Michael, and their two children, Christopher and Amanda.

Ruth Senter is best described as a true reflective thinker who can turn the ordinary events of life into memorable insights about God. Complementing Ruth's introspective abilities is a delightful sense of humor and a contagious sense of joy about life and people. Ruth and her husband, Mark, who is Dean of Continuing Education at Trinity Evangelical Divinity School, Deerfield, Illinois, reside in Wheaton, Illinois. Currently, Ruth serves as Senior Editor of *Campus Life* magazine. She is the author of eight books, including *The Seasons of Friendship* (Zondervan) and her most recent book, *When You're On Your Own: Ten Things Every Young Woman Needs to Know As She Faces an Adult World* (Zondervan).

We should strive for a quality in our friendships that parallels the story Ruth told of a man who once interviewed the prime minister of England. "After the interview the journalist was asked what it was like to interview the prime minister. He thought for a minute and said, 'I've interviewed rich and famous people all over the world, and I usually come away from the interviews thinking what a great person he or she is. Today, I walked out of the prime minister's office and thought to myself, *What a great person I am.*' Somehow the prime minister, in what he said or did, evoked in the heart of this journalist a sense of contentment with himself," explains Ruth. It is this kind of excitement and attitude we need to bring out in one another through our friendships.

———— ∽ ————

It's been said, "To have a good friend is one of the highest delights of life; to be a good friend is one of the noblest and most difficult undertakings." Can we hope to have those close bonds with others much like the apostle Paul had with Titus—that friend who could refresh and comfort him during times of hardship (2 Corinthians 6–7)?

The answer is "yes," for we can be confident that the God who created us and loves us surely placed others in our lives to help us grow, tend to our spiritual needs, comfort us in times of trouble, and encourage us. May this book open up the avenues for you to healthy, rewarding, and lasting friendships.

Marian V. Liautaud and
Louise A. Ferrebee, Editors

PART ONE

MASTERING THE BASICS

WHILE WE MIGHT have learned the basics of friendship in kindergarten—don't hit, share your toys, be nice—as adults we can attest that relationships involve more than following a few simple rules. As women designed by our Creator with certain nurturing and relational gifts, our need for friendship is complex. Our expectations are often high. Our desire to reach out and be connected through friendship runs much deeper than the childhood plea, "I need someone to play with."

How do we develop those friendships like the one described in Proverbs 18:24, "There are 'friends' who pretend to be friends, but there is a friend who sticks closer than a brother" (TLB)? If a single word could sum up the key to successful friendship—a word frequently repeated by each contributor—that word would be intentional. We must reach out and make friendship a priority.

The building blocks to rewarding friendship are something to which we each have access—the ability to make and keep a commitment and the use of our time and energy. As Colleen and Stormie note, friendship begins with you. Here's how to polish those friendship skills and become confident in the basics that lead to lasting friendships.

1

What Are the Foundations of a Good Friendship?

—*Colleen Evans*

WE'VE ALL HEARD the saying, "To have a good friend you must be a good friend." But just what *is* a good friend? What are some reasonable expectations of what we should bring to a friendship and what we should expect in return? While we each are unique individuals with varying needs and expectations, there are several elements that are essential for any deep and growing friendship to prosper.

First of all, we need to realize that friendship is a kind of work. It's joyful work, but nonetheless work because the making of a good friendship is a conscious choice on behalf of two people. Beyond that, it involves intentional action on the part of each person. In our journey toward genuine friendship these intentional actions are to *know*, to *care*, and to *remember*. As we spend time with a person we naturally get to know them—we share our personal history, our birthday, our interests. I often want a snapshot of my friend to stick on the refrigerator or bulletin board. From the knowledge we gain about one another, we then make an effort to remember those things that matter in the inner world of the other person.

I have one friend who loves bunnies, so whenever I

see a bunny, whether it's on a greeting card or in a toy department, I always think of her and, if it's possible and appropriate, I buy it for her. *Remembering* may not come readily but it's essential to a friendship because it shows you care. One friend of mine is naturally thoughtful—she remembers so many things about her friends. I'm learning from her the importance of remembering little things—even something as simple as an anniversary or a birthday.

I once said to her, "I can't remember all those dates. How do you do it?" Her secret was to keep a book listing those important dates. I finally did the same thing, and while it may sound corny, that little birthday book sure works. It helps me remember those "little things" about the people I feel God wants me to be intentional about.

It's a Two-Way Street

Besides the intentional actions of knowing, caring, and remembering another person, it's important in any deep and growing friendship for a *mutuality* to exist. In other words, a truly deep friendship won't be lopsided. Rather, each person in the friendship will be able to lean on the other—the nurturing attitude will go both ways.

Mary Jane, my very close friend who is a marriage and family therapist, described this mutuality well when she said, "A healthy, balanced friendship is one in which the interests of both are focused in turn on the life experiences of both." Friendship is a two-way street.

Now, I'm not saying we *can't* have some friendships that are lopsided for a while—a friend might need us more than we need *them* during a crisis. And there are times when God leads us to someone who needs us in a specific way for a specific time—maybe right after the birth of a child. I've certainly been in that position in my life—especially when I had four children age five and under. I needed more help than I could give in those years. Such situations are not a misuse of friendship as long as both people agree to focus the energy of their relationship one way. However, such one-way relationships that never grow toward mutuality aren't likely to evolve into long-term, growing friendships. For that to happen, over time there needs to be a more equal amount of give-and-take in the friendship.

Please Step Aside

One primary way we get to know a person and show we care is through listening. And listening, one of the key characteristics of a good relationship, is most successful when we are able to lay ourselves aside. However, putting another person first is an intentional action that takes discipline.

E IS FOR EFFORT

Without intentional effort an acquaintance isn't truly a friendship—it's more of a happening. Such a friendship is like a balloon floating through the air, subject to the haphazard currents of the wind. It's fragile and when it gets too high it will eventually burst. Intentional effort is what builds solid, lasting relationships.

—Ruth

We've all been in the position at some time or another of meeting someone new. Naturally, we're eager to make a good impression and as a result it's hard for us to lay ourselves aside. During the conversation, we're often thinking of what we'll say next. We're "loading our guns while the other person is talking," as someone once described it. So, the person isn't getting our full attention, we aren't really listening, and as a result we can't remember what that person said. One reason I don't remember what's important to a certain person is because too often I'm thinking about myself and how I'm being perceived rather than listening to that person.

When we lay ourselves aside, we can tune in to the feelings behind what is said and not just hear the words. I've found that the feeling behind the words is more important than the words themselves. I once read that six percent of our communication is verbal—the rest is body language, tone of voice, or look in the eye.

For me, putting myself second is a spiritual discipline of sorts. When I'm going to be with someone, I'll pray beforehand, asking God's help in keeping my focus on that person instead of myself. I love people, and I'm naturally interested—even curious—about people, but I need God's help to *listen* to them—to really *hear* what they are saying and sense what they are feeling.

Are You Building Each Other Up?

Another fundamental element of true friendship is that a friend accepts you as you are—she isn't out to change you. While each of us will have certain shortcomings, as friends we should be willing to overlook them. After all, who's perfect?

However, honesty is important, and we shouldn't overlook a fault if it is hindering our friend's walk with Christ. But before we can offer a word of warning or admonition, we have to *earn* the right to be honest with our friend. A level of genuine affection and trust that is built over time must exist before we are given permission to speak the truth in love.

Unfortunately, some people are so intent on fixing others that they barge in, say their piece, and then retreat. Frankly, I'm not ready to hear that kind of honest talk from someone unless they've been alongside me for a while and are planning to stick with me for a long time to come. Then I'm not only willing to hear what they have to say, but I'm grateful for that kind of accountability in our relationship.

The main work of a friendship is not to fix one another but to affirm and encourage one another, and when we do see a weakness, we need to ask, "Can I fill that gap? Is there something I can do for my friend in that area?"

While we should expect our friends to accept us unconditionally, we should likewise expect them to help us see our positives—to identify our strengths and build on the good that exists.

For example, a close friend and I get away for an afternoon or a whole day, if possible, just before we're about to enter a new season in our lives, whether it be a momentous birthday, a transition in our family, a move, or a new work experience that will alter our lives. During our time together we'll probe each other with questions like, "What do you think God is asking you to do in this season? What do you want to do? What are the gifts you're to use at this time?" As each of us talks we write down what the other says. It always amazes me how much focus this brings to our lives.

With our list in hand, we then know what to say "yes" or "no" to in the coming season. Beyond that we try to keep one another accountable for how we use our gifts and strengths as we seek to be obedient to God's plan for a new season.

Besides my one friend helping me in this way, author Catherine Marshall used to do much the same for me. If she knew I was working on a book project, she would call at certain intervals and ask, "Coke, are you *abiding* in your call?" When she put it that way, I knew I couldn't make any excuses, because if I did, she would respond, "If you felt that was what God meant for you to do, nothing is more important than that."

We must make the conscious choice to say, "I'm going to focus on the good things in you, my friend." The world loves darkness rather than light, and when we get hooked on the negatives we can't see the positives. Not that we should be Pollyannas but rather, we need to say, "I see great gifts and potential in you and I'd like to help you discover them."

——————— ❧ ———————

Besides accepting each other unconditionally and focusing on the positives, another ingredient to true friendship is a sense that you are cheerleaders for each other. We need to bring to the relationship a sense of loyalty that isn't dependent upon performance. Even though we may goof up at times we need to know our friends are always in our corner.

In my close friendships I like to know that I can tell a friend something without the fear she'll say, "That does it. I'm out of here." A friend gives you the benefit of the doubt just as God does with us. Not that God winks at sin, but rather He calls it what it is and gives us a second chance.

There's a wonderful verse in Proverbs 17:17 that says, "A friend loves at all times, and a brother [or sister] is born for adversity." In other words, true friends are faithful in times of adversity—they hang in there when the going gets tough.

TAKE THE RISK

We should be willing to lay down our lives for a friend—in terms of personal sacrifice—and be willing to risk that the friendship might not last very long. When you say "no" to friendship you cheat yourself and the Lord. In John 15:12, Jesus says, "My command is this: Love each other as I have loved you." That's the kind of love we need to bring to a friendship.

—Stormie

During our days in Washington, D.C., we saw many people who would eagerly support and associate themselves with a certain politician—that is, until something would go wrong—say a possible investigation into his finances or an ethics charge. When that happened these so-called friends quickly fell away.

Louie and I saw this happen often, and it grieved us. As a result, we made a conscious decision to move in the opposite direction. If a friend of ours was going through a tough time we would come alongside. Rather than distance ourselves, we'd press in closer.

We should expect the same in our friendships. I don't think you'll be a good friend or have a close friend unless this kind of loyalty exists. When we stumble and fall, when we make a mistake, we need to know without a doubt our friend is in there pulling for us.

Blessed With Variety

We are complex people, and the more complex we are the greater diversity we can expect in our friendships. Different friends fill different needs in our lives, and likewise, we can expect to fill different needs in the lives of our friends. We should never expect one person to meet all of our friendship needs—just imagine the burden that would put on us or the other individual. Besides, one person was never created to bear such a burden that rightfully belongs *only* to God. Only God can meet *all* of our needs, and one of the ways God meets our needs is to give us a variety of people in our lives.

Some time ago a psychologist came to the church where we were serving to do a team-building exercise with the entire staff, including me. Upon reading my test results, the psychologist said, "You're a closet hippie because you like so many *different* kinds of people." It's true that I have a wide variety of friends.

For instance, I have one friend who shares my passion for helping the poor and ministering in the inner-city. It was this common interest that brought us together as we worked in the urban ghettos of Washington, D.C.

I have another friend whom I call my "play friend." She's a wonderful Christian woman with a playful nature, and she is forever thinking up fun things to do. I, too, love to play, but I tend to focus more on ministry and my "let's change the world" attitude. I need those playful, fun-loving friends in my life to bring balance.

When we both turned fifty, my "play friend" said, "We should do something that we've always wanted to do but have never had the courage to do. What is it?"

"I've always wanted to learn how to tap dance," I said.

Her response was, "Me, too! Let's *do* it!"

Together we signed up for weekly tap dancing lessons, and for nearly a year we had the most hilarious time. We got pretty good until our teacher announced she was going to hold a recital. When we realized that meant we'd have to invite our families to watch us "brush-tap-tap" across the stage dressed in "leo-tights," our tap dancing career ended . . . fast!

Limited Circle of Friends

As Christians we know we are to care about everyone, but where we trip up is in assuming we should be friends with everyone. That's impossible. Genuine friendship, based on *knowing, caring,* and *remembering* a person, takes time and energy, and we are limited in those resources. Now, we can value all the people God places in our lives—we can pray for them and love them—but we can't expect to form true friendships with everyone.

Jesus, while on earth, had to deal with the same constraints we do, and He offered a perfect model of friendship in the process. First of all, Jesus, by the way He lived His life, gives us permission to develop deep friendships with a small handful of people. He chose twelve men to be with Him, and I believe the twelve weren't chosen *only* to build the kingdom of God, but for *companionship* as well. Jesus wanted company! Of the twelve there were three He was especially close to, and out of the three there was one known as the disciple Jesus loved—John.

Beyond the twelve, Jesus had many others he related to in special ways such as Mary, Martha, and Lazarus. But Jesus was limited by time when he walked the earth—just like we are. Like us, He couldn't have deep friendships with everyone. *Knowing this helps me in setting my expectations for friendship.*

When we were in seminary, years ago, we were strongly discouraged from having close friends once we began serving in a church. Though the message has since changed, during our seminary days we lived by the code "A pastor and his wife should show no partiality—everyone must be treated the same." Thankfully, and I think wisely, Louie and I didn't adhere to this advice because while we could care and love each member of the congregation, like Jesus, we needed more. We needed *close* friends. So, there were those with whom we shared a special chemistry and those whom we needed to hold us accountable and support us. It was in covenant relationships that we invested much of our energy and time, and because of these brothers and sisters in our lives we will never be the same!

What we want *from* friendship we need to bring *to* the friendship. If one word sums up what makes for a deep, growing friendship it would be the word *intentional.* Friendship is by no means passive—it takes action on our part to know, to care, and to remember. It takes effort to listen, to lay ourselves aside, to give as much as we take. And when we do follow through on these intentional actions, when the chemistry between two people is right, then we are blessed with a great sense of joy, appreciation, and gratitude for those special relationships God makes possible in our lives.

Make It Happen

1. List your expectations for friendship. Lay the list aside for a few days and read 1 Samuel 18–19, which describes the friendship between David and Jonathan. Meditate on what you've read and in a few days go back to the list of your expectations for friendship. Are they realistic? Are they biblical? Are some of them more self-centered than other-centered? With prayer, adjust your expectations.

2. How would you rate your friendship skills? In need of polishing? Doing well but could be better with a few adjustments? Friendships don't just happen—they take putting your friendship skills to work on a continual basis. If you're not pleased with some of your skills, or you see skills in others that you'd like to incorporate into your life, take the time to do that. The rewards will be worth the effort.

3. Take a minute and mentally list the friendships in your life. Have you spread yourself too thin? Remember, we have limited time and energy to give to knowing, caring, and remembering someone. If we're trying to be friends with too many people, then chances are we're shortchanging our friendships.

A Model Friend
Dee Brestin

The name "Ruth" literally means "a woman friend." And the Ruth of the Old Testament shows us the depth of friendship women are capable of if we use our gift for intimacy in obedience to God. Ruth's example encourages us to be the kind of friend God longs for us to be. Here's how.

Ruth valued friendship with other women. There's a dramatic contrast between Naomi and her daughter-in-law Ruth. When Naomi lost her husband and sons, God tried to minister to her through Ruth, but Naomi couldn't accept it. Naomi told Ruth she was foolishly hurting her chances for finding another husband.

But Ruth valued men and women equally. She left her chances for remarriage in God's hands and stood by Naomi.

Ruth committed herself to restore Naomi. In the beginning of the story, Naomi, whose name means "pleasant," asked her friends to call her "Mara," or "bitter." There doesn't seem to be anything pleasant about Naomi.

But Ruth remembered a different Naomi, and was determined to restore her. Despite the fact that Naomi ordered her to return to Moab, Ruth remained steadfast. Wedding music composers would have us believe these words were spoken by a bride to her groom, but in reality they were spoken by one woman friend to another: "Entreat me not to leave thee, or to turn away from following after thee; for whither thou goest, I will go and where thou lodgest, I will lodge; thy people shall be my people, and thy God, my God" (Ruth 1:16–17, KJV).

In keeping these words, Ruth modeled how to help a grieving friend. She didn't criticize, she didn't offer advice—she simply sat with Naomi and quietly loved her. And it is through Ruth's faithfulness that Naomi finally caught a glimmer of God's goodness again.

Ruth was not easily offended. One unfortunate side effect of our sensitivity is that women tend to be thin-skinned. Despite Ruth's commitment to stay with her, Naomi seemed unmoved. Instead of thanking Ruth for her steadfastness, Naomi turned on her heel and walked to Bethlehem. I suspect she was thinking, "What I need is a man—not this young girl!"

When the two got to Bethlehem, Naomi told her friends she went away full, but came back empty. Ruth was standing right at her side! How that must have hurt!

How did Ruth react? She covered Naomi's unkindness with love, understood her pain, and persisted in being helpful, kind, good.

Even Christian women often trust in their relationships rather than in God. We sometimes tend to cling to others. But Ruth was amazing. When her husband died, she undoubtedly grieved, but she clung to God. And although she cherished Naomi and committed herself to her, she was not dependent on her or devastated by her lack of appreciation. Ruth looked to God for her strength. She was in God's hands, and was completely convinced He does all things well.

At the end of the story, Naomi's neighbors rebuked her, saying, "Your daughter-in-law, who loves you . . . is better to you than seven sons" (Ruth 4:15).

And she was.

—From *Today's Christian Woman* (March/April 1990)

2

How Do I Develop Close, Intimate Friendships?

—Colleen Evans

THERE'S A SPECIAL CHEMISTRY between me and a dear friend I've had since our days in La Jolla, California. Whenever Honni and I get together and drive somewhere, we inevitably miss stops and exits because we become so absorbed in talking to each other we forget where we're going. As we turn around and head in the right direction, we laugh and promise ourselves, "We won't let this happen again." But of course, it does.

In my lifetime, I've had many friends, but those with whom I've formed close and intimate friendships—like my friend Honni—are indeed rare. I can count on my hands those people in my life whom I feel totally accepted and loved by, at one with, and willing to give my life for. I consider these friendships a great blessing— treasures in my life.

While deep friendships are a combination of work and chemistry, the primary ingredient for any relationship to develop from a casual acquaintance into a close, intimate friendship is a step *we* must choose to take.

Dare to Be Transparent

During our years in Washington, D.C., Louie and I were involved in what is known as a covenant group

33

ministry within the church. In the beginning, several groups were set up for the purpose of spiritual growth. As time passed, other groups came together more spontaneously. Ours was a group of six couples, and together we made a covenant—a promise—to love and support one another on a regular basis through prayer and availability. We also agreed, in matters of faith and life, to hold one another accountable. We belonged to that covenant group all the years we served in Washington, and we continue to share our lives as we travel across the country two to three times a year to be together. Our group is convinced that an essential part of our closeness is a willingness to be transparent with our emotions, our ideas, and our lives.

Early in our group's history, one way we encouraged transparency was by asking questions of each other. While it might have seemed a bit gimmicky, it worked. For instance, one time we asked, "What do you fear most at this point in your life?" We were all surprised when one of our members shared that she was a diabetic—news to all of us because she so carefully covered it up. Several times a day she had to inject herself with insulin and check her blood sugar. Her greatest fear was that something might happen to her husband who was not only her lover and friend, but also her medical coach. "Bill watches everything. I don't know what I'd do without him," she said. "Whenever he's late getting home from work or I hear a siren, my heart tightens because I not only love him, but in a very physical way, I *need* him."

Her eyes filled with tears, and we realized that we knew something about her that we'd never known before—something that wasn't obvious to other people. Her answer was very revealing and allowed us inside her innermost thoughts. We loved her for that vulnerability.

Once the foundation of a friendship is formed and a certain level of trust exists, we allow ourselves to grow increasingly transparent by revealing more about ourselves over time. In a sense, you test the waters. You don't suddenly jump in, totally unveil yourself and say, "Here I am; take me or leave me." Rather, bit-by-bit you reveal yourself and your friend does likewise. As you share your inner thoughts and feelings, if what you say is accepted, you take another step and then another. Intimacy in friendship is a process.

While transparency is vital for a deep, growing friendship to develop, some people make the mistake of revealing too much too fast. A friend who immediately dumps her innermost thoughts too quickly puts another in the position of a counselor rather than a friend. The mutuality I talked about in the last chapter—that equal give-and-take—doesn't have a chance to happen.

IN HIS HANDS

You can't force someone to be your friend, so when I meet someone I really want to be friends with I start praying for her. I pray for her in every way I can think I would want her to be blessed, and then I pray for the Lord to open up the doors of friendship. Some of my closest friendships have started out like this, and I credit the Lord for allowing such friendships to develop.

—Stormie

This type of lopsided transparency often happens to people in the public eye. As an author, I've had someone say to me, "I just read your book and I feel like I know you. Can I talk to you about something?" As the person begins to pour out her heart, I have learned to sit back and say to myself, "This is going to be one of those counseling-type relationships where both our energies are focused on the one person." That's fine under those circumstances. In fact, I have come to consider sharing another's life in that way a privilege, but I know that such a relationship will most likely never lead to a close friendship.

In a rare mix of chemistry you might be able to develop a certain closeness with another person in just a few contacts. Something clicks, and the friendship takes minimal effort. More often than not, however, a close, intimate friendship takes time. And just as a friendship requires *quality* time together, the *quantity* of time together counts as well. You need to see each other with some degree of regularity because without consistent contact you can find yourself sharing only superficial news when you do meet. While such surface talk is important, if all your time is spent catching up on the details of life then that leaves little time for sharing nitty-gritty feelings.

When several of us from our covenant group would meet for lunch, we'd usually start with the question, "How are you?" Naturally, we'd talk about our husbands and the kids. Soon, someone would chime in, "Now I want to know how *you* are—not your family." We'd then share at another deeper level. And before too long, someone would ask, "Okay, now how are you *really*?" In other words, "How is your soul—deep-down inside?"

Now, we could stop at each level of sharing and be somewhat satisfied, but for a truly intimate friendship we need to go to that third level—the one that requires self-revelation of our real thoughts and feelings. It takes work, patience, and persistence to reach that level but without it, it's unlikely we'll develop a close and intimate friendship.

Intimacy Means Taking a Risk

When my children were young, a friend of mine who is single looked at them adoringly and said, "It must be so wonderful to have children." Without too much thought or sensitivity I replied, "You'll have your own family one day, too."

"Oh, no," she assured me. "I'm *never* going to get married. I'm not going to take that risk."

Today, my friend is still single. My children are grown and have children of their own. I'm convinced my friend will never marry and have a family for the simple reason she told me, "I'll never take the risk—if you love that much you can be hurt that much as well."

The transparency that leads to true intimacy between people involves taking a risk. Like my friend, many of us hesitate to be transparent out of fear. When we reveal ourselves as we truly are there is the chance we will be rejected because of what we say and, consequently, we may be hurt by that rejection.

We stop ourselves from being transparent when we think, "If someone really knows how I feel, possibly they won't love me." We hold our thoughts inside when we question a friend's loyalty and trust, wondering, "Is she really in my corner, or does her love come with strings attached?" And who hasn't worried that upon sharing our needs and pain, the response will be, "So what?"

I've been hurt loads of times in close relationships, but rather than saying, "I'm never going to venture out again because I've been hurt," I've learned to say, "Maybe I trusted the wrong person. Okay, so I made a mistake! Maybe this wasn't the right mix." In those situations, my prayer has been, "God, give me the gift of discernment. Lead me to the people that I can trust . . . and keep me trusting."

What allows me to do this, and what allows all Christians to risk rejection, is the fact our self-image and concept doesn't rest on one person rejecting or accepting us.

Rather, our self-image—our security—is in Christ. The fact that He created us and loves us, values us—that's security.

Bill and Gloria Gaither wrote a song called, "I Am Loved," that says, "I am loved. I am loved. I can risk loving you. For the One who knows me best, loves me most."* When we have that kind of love available to us from God then we can take the risk of being transparent.

Besides this confidence that allows us to venture out and reveal our true feelings, we can also trust God to help us move beyond our pain if we are hurt by rejection. And remember, even good friends have misunderstandings and experience pain. We must learn to trust God with all our emotions, knowing that when we do get hurt He is big enough to heal us. We are all going to be hurt at some point in our friendships—it goes with the territory. If you take the risk of caring, you take the risk of being hurt as well. But God can heal the hurt and enable us to forgive and move on.

I have a friend who was deeply hurt when she and her husband were maligned by another couple at church. Since that time, my friend has erected a wall around herself. Sure, she's gracious, kind, and loving up to a point, but she says, "Never again will I allow anyone into my heart." She admits, "I'm not ready to forgive yet. I just can't let go." Sadly, my friend is cheating herself and others.

We have so much to gain when we take the risk of being transparent. The door is open to true intimacy in our friendships, and we can live a life beyond a superficial level. While we can choose to avoid risk and rejection, the price is often a lonely, empty life.

Remember, it takes courage to risk and to trust—especially when you've been disappointed a few times. But

---

*"I Am Loved" words by William J. and Gloria Gaither. Music by William J. Gaither. Copyright © 1978 by William J. Gaither. All rights reserved. Used by permission.

I believe God means for us to be transparent whether or not we are taken seriously, whether or not we are rejected. If we shirk back from living, simply because it might bring pain, then we are saying "no" to life and to God.

In the book *God In the Dark* (Zondervan), poet Luci Shaw described how, after the death of her husband, some friends were able to minister to her in a way unlike any other friends. I know that is true in my life as well. In my times of need there are certain people I call and other good friends that I don't call. Not that my good friends don't care or wouldn't understand, but rather those soul-mates in my life understand in a way unlike anyone else. I know that my pain is their pain as well.

Worth the Effort

God created us with an innate desire for relationships so that we could give expression to the love we feel. To me, a life without a friend to whom you can pour out your heart is a life of poverty. If you don't have a close friendship with someone, then make that the growing edge in your life—an area where you're willing to put forth some effort. It's easy to say, "I'm just not good at close relationships," or "I can't give the time to such friendships."

If you don't have a close friendship with at least one person in your life (and remember, husbands count) pray today, "God, show me why I don't." Then ask yourself, "Am I willing to be transparent?" "Am I willing to give-and-take?" "Am I willing to risk?" If the answer is "no," find the reasons why you hesitate to risk sharing your feelings and your life with others.

Even if you are by nature a very reserved, quiet person there will most likely be one person who can pull you out—someone with whom your spirit resonates. With the right person, each of us has the ability to be transparent. What we need is confidence that if our eyes

39

and hearts are open, God will bring the right people into our lives.

———— ✑ ————

The closeness that exists in a deep friendship is to a degree a mystery. Why is there a chemistry between some people and not others? I often think it's because the Holy Spirit creates a special link between us. While covenant relationships and deep friendships require commitment, most intimate relationships can't be planned. There is a serendipity to such friendships.

AN INVISIBLE SPARK

A large percentage of friendship is chemistry—it's an intangible. For as much as you can evaluate and critique a friendship for the reasons it exists, often it boils down to an invisible spark between two people.

—Ruth

I once saw a poster that read, "Be of love more careful than anything." To that I would add, "Once you find it in a treasured friend, treat her most carefully" for she is indeed a precious and rare gift.

Make It Happen

1. Think back to your earliest childhood memories of friendship. Did you have a soul-mate growing up? In your college years? What made that friendship so special? If you haven't been able to keep in touch, don't be filled with regrets but instead look for such a friendship within your current contacts.

2. If you're currently without a close, intimate friend

then examine yourself. Is it a case of timing, or is the reason behind this lack in your life of your own doing? With open and honest communication between you and the Lord, ask for insights into what you need to change to make space for someone special within your heart. Then give yourself time to change certain traits that need changing.

3. Consider forming a covenant group in your church. It can begin with women who have seasons of life, interests, or careers in common. Lay the foundations for the type of deep and close friendship within the parameters of a covenant group.

3

What Role Should My Faith Play in the Friends I Choose?

—Stormie Omartian

SINCE HIGH SCHOOL DAYS, Diane and I were best friends. She knew everything about me—the abuse I endured as a child raised by a mentally ill mother, my difficult teenage years, the struggles I faced as a young adult trying to cope with the effects of a frightening childhood. Diane understood because she experienced a similar dysfunctional family situation.

At age twenty-eight I hit rock bottom. I didn't want to live anymore—suicide appeared to be the only answer. Around the time I decided to end my life, Terry, a Christian friend, called me to sing background for a recording session. During a break she mentioned that I seemed depressed and suggested I go with her to meet her pastor, someone she seemed certain could help me. I figured, "What have I got to lose?"

Together we met with Pastor Jack, as Terry called him, and the three of us talked for nearly two hours. Then Pastor Jack gave me three books to read—one by C. S. Lewis, a book on the Holy Spirit, and, finally, the Book of John. These books had a profound effect on me and a week later, when we all met again to discuss the books, Pastor Jack led me in prayer, and I accepted Christ. Although I didn't understand everything that had happened, I left feeling like a new person.

While my lifelong friend Diane had understood my suffering and challenges, she hadn't been able to offer me a solution to my problems. She was not a believer and so had never experienced the life-changing renewal I had, nor did she understand me when I talked about it. A sort of emptiness began to grow between us.

Making the Circle Complete

As I discovered, a friendship with a non-Christian is always going to be incomplete. It will never be the fulfilling, deep relationship you want it to be until your friend comes to know the same God you do. While Diane and I continued to talk to each other, there was a level— a spiritual level—we simply couldn't communicate on. As someone involved with New Age practices, Diane couldn't understand my enthusiasm, my excitement, or the depth of the relationship I had with a living God. My relationship with Jesus was a major part of my life and yet my best friend couldn't share in it.

I prayed continually for Diane's salvation. Fortunately, about three years after I received Jesus, Diane also was saved. It happened suddenly one day as we talked on the phone. She opened up, shared some of her deepest feelings, and I led her to the Lord. Once Diane accepted Christ, the bond between us deepened. We prayed together over the phone early in the morning, at least three times a week. Diane grew to become a true woman of God with great spiritual insights and revelations.

I'm not certain where our friendship would have led if Diane hadn't eventually accepted the Lord. Early on, the fact I had become a Christian and she hadn't caused a major breach in our friendship—without a common belief, something significant was missing in our relationship.

Shared faith plays an important role in our deepest

friendships. As Christians, I believe our relationships should be consecrated to the Lord and bring glory to God. And that's a difficult order to fill when one friend believes and the other doesn't.

While we can and should have non-Christian friends, we must realize that we'll carry with us a continual ache in our hearts for them. If we truly hope to bring glory to God through that friendship, then we'll want the best for our friend—to know Jesus. If we really care for a friend, we'll be concerned about where she is going to spend eternity.

A Light in the Darkness

Looking back, I never forgot the Christians I met during my non-Christian days. These people affected me in a special way—Mrs. Anderson, my high school teacher who talked about the Christlike way to live; Jimmy Owens, the gospel songwriter who asked me to sing on his recording sessions; Terry, the young woman who always spoke boldly about Jesus (and later introduced me to the pastor who led me to the Lord). While I didn't want anything to do with Christianity then, I never forgot these people or what they had shared with me. When the time came to reflect, I put together all that I'd noticed about them—I remembered a quality I liked in each person, and the common denominator was that the Spirit of God was alive in their hearts.

If you share anything of the Lord with a non-Christian, in some way it touches her. Like me, someday your friend will add it up and say, "I like those qualities I see in her," and recognize Christ shining through.

A Christian who is friends with a non-Christian can positively touch that person's life. I know my personal input and intercession for Diane was a major factor in her coming to the Lord. If I had chosen to drop our friendship, I don't know of anyone else who would have prayed for her salvation. I don't think she knew another believer other than me.

ONE DOOR CLOSES, ANOTHER OPENS

When I transferred from one high school to another my sophomore year I desperately wanted to fit in with the popular group. That didn't exactly happen the way I'd hoped. Instead I became friends with some Christian kids. I'm the person I am today because of those friends. Because I let go of some of the friendships I thought I had to have, I came out of high school with strong Christian principles and some strong Christian friendships which have lasted to this day.

—Ruth

All this isn't to say our *only* reason for maintaining friendships with non-Christians is to bring them into the kingdom—to add another notch in the post. Not all friendships will lead to someone accepting Christ. But a natural outgrowth of caring for someone will be concern for her salvation.

My manicurist, Vickie, was a non-Christian when I first met her, so I prayed for her as I did for Diane. I liked her as a friend and wanted to enjoy her fellowship in God's family, but, more important, I didn't want her to spend eternity separated from God. The wonderful privilege of leading her into the kingdom was worth the effort it took.

———— ✍ ————

While it hasn't always been the case, at this particular point in my life, all of my immediate friends are Christians. They were not all believers when I first met them, but thankfully they didn't stay that way. Surprisingly though, I miss having a non-Christian friend. Non-believers help us keep our evangelism tools sharp because they ask questions about our faith that challenge us to reevaluate exactly where we stand. If you find someone you like who isn't a Christian, don't shy away from a friendship with her. Accept the challenge that this kind of friendship can offer. As your relationship develops you can bless your friend with your love, kindness, and knowledge of the goodness of the Lord. A friendship that grows you in the Lord is part of God's plan for restoration. Just as I was able to be restored through the love of God and people like Terry, now it's my turn to be an instrument of restoration for someone else.

Friendships with non-Christians will always challenge us to grow. I know mine have. With both Vickie and Diane, I learned patience and perseverance. Kindness and love were also being refined in me. When these traits are evident in a friendship, then the relationship brings glory to the Lord. However, if friendship with a non-Christian doesn't exhibit any of these traits, perhaps it's time to stop and examine your motives for the friendship.

A Word of Caution

When it comes to relationships with non-Christians we need to use discretion and discernment. Such friendships can be rewarding, but we need to be especially prayerful about whom we befriend. If you're in a situation where most of your friends are non-Christian, you have to be careful not to compromise what you know is right. As it says in Romans 12:2, "Do not conform any longer to the pattern of this world, but be transformed by the renewing of your mind."

As Christians, we walk a fine line in our friendships with non-Christians. We want to hold to what is right, yet not appear to be judgmental. We want to show love, not legalism. We must live what we believe and not allow unrighteousness or impurity into our lives because when we do, it begins to erode our Christian walk in subtle ways. The barometer I suggest is if you are a godly influence in your friend's life, the friendship is good. If she is an ungodly influence in your life, you'd be better off to find another friendship in which God is glorified.

FORGIVE AND FORGET

The most notable difference between my Christian and non-Christian friends is that the non-Christians don't have the same understanding of forgiveness. My Christian friends operate on grace. When I say, "Oops, I goofed," I'm forgiven and the incident is forgotten. With my non-Christian friends they simply can't comprehend the fact that I forgive and forget when they goof. They keep bringing the incident up and have trouble moving on.

—Colleen

My friend Vickie experienced the subtle pull of a non-Christian friend shortly after she joined the church. As a young, single woman, Vickie got involved with a handsome man who worked at a bank. He appeared to be good "marriage material," but it soon became evident her relationship with this man wasn't bringing glory to God. The man pulled her away from church, away from God. But Vickie was blinded—she couldn't see beyond this man's sharp suits and smooth talk. Her heart became hard to the things of God, and one Sunday when the congregation was moved to tears by the message, she said, "I didn't get a thing out of the sermon." I ached for her.

Gradually, she stopped going to church, and soon after that her life fell apart and she became physically sick. When her boyfriend eventually left her, she hit bottom and came back to the Lord. I asked her to examine the fruit of that relationship. "Think about all that happened to you," I said. "Did he lead you closer to God or further away?"

In our friendships with non-Christians we need to assess the fruit that grows out of the relationship. What positive qualities or traits are we developing because of our friendship? Vickie has since met a nice man, and while they might not be destined for the altar, this man takes her to church, reads the Word, prays with her, and points her mind in a godly direction.

Looking for a Few Good Women

As Christians, we should strive for those deepest and closest friendships to be with fellow believers. Like it says in Proverbs 27:17, "As iron sharpens iron, so one man sharpens another." Among my Christian friends, we each provide positive input into each other's lives. Our friendship strengthens our individual walk with God, and together we help each other overcome emotional hurts that keep us from experiencing the fullness of God's love.

I tend to be attracted to people who are truly dedicated to the Lord. Yet, while I admire someone who is spiritually grown up in the Lord, I also seek out friendships with Christians whose faith is less developed. For me it's important to strike a balance between friends who can further lead me in my faith and friends whom I can help lead.

———— ✑ ————

If you're surrounded by non-Christians and that's the pool you have for making friendships, ask the Lord for a Christian friend. He will provide one. It's almost as though He brings Christians out of the woodwork in places you'd least expect. It might be someone at the grocery store or, as I discovered, in the beauty salon. It always amazes me how the Lord will specifically answer prayer.

After I accepted the Lord, most of my non-Christian friends deserted me—they thought I had really lost my mind. For a while, I didn't have Christian friends either—only acquaintances. It was a difficult transition, but as I prayed for good Christian friends, God brought me the finest. God puts spiritually sensitive people in your life and before you know it, you've developed valuable friendships.

———— ∞ ————

A common faith offers a strong foundation for a friendship because it unites you with another person on every level of your being. While friendships with non-Christians are possible, and even important, they will never be complete.

I was still friends with Diane after I received the Lord, but I could never rest in my spirit knowing I was going to heaven and she wasn't. Thankfully, God used our friendship as a way to bring Diane into the kingdom. Now she's in heaven with Him, and I am so thankful that one day I'll see her again.

Make It Happen

1. Examine your list of current close friends. Do you tend to have more non-Christian friends than Christian friends? Do your Christian friends represent a variety of levels spiritually—are there some that challenge you, some that you can help along? Remember, this kind of balance is important.

2. Is there someone in your life right now who could

benefit from the knowledge you've gained in your spiritual journey? Without being too presumptuous, be attuned in your contacts in or out of church for that one person God wants you to encourage along.

3. If your closest friendships are with non-Christians, make it a point to pray for a Christian friend. While your friendships may be meeting many of your needs, as a growing Christian it's vital that our deepest bonds be with those who share our faith. The level of friendship between sisters in Christ is a bond that can't be beat.

When a Friend Isn't a Christian
Dee Brestin

When I introduced my children to the woman who was my best friend in childhood and the maid of honor at my wedding, their mouths hung open.

I understood my children's reaction, for if I were to meet Hilary for the first time now, I would probably assume we could never be best friends. And she might categorize me as one of those "crazy born-again Christians" and give me a wide berth.

Hilary is not a Christian. She is a free spirit who lives in a log cabin in the mountains of Oregon. She has never married and is currently living with a man fourteen years her junior.

On the other hand, I received Christ when our firstborn was a baby. I am a homemaker, wife, and mother of five in Nebraska. But despite our differences, I love Hilary like a sister, and wish with all my heart she shared the most precious part of my life—my faith.

One week this past summer, for the first time in two years, we were reunited at the lake where our parents both owned cottages. I hoped that during our time together Hilary would show some interest in Jesus.

One morning, as we walked along the beach, I asked her what she thought about Jesus. She answered reluctantly, and finally told me she didn't want to talk about religion anymore. I didn't want to erect an impenetrable barrier between us, so I respected her request and we walked along the beach in silence.

Although Hilary doesn't embrace my faith in Christ, I love her dearly and I will not give up on her. Our friendship bond is too strong and too precious to sever.

My relationship with Hilary, and with other non-Christians, has taught me some principles that may help you relate to your non-Christian friends.

1. Despite the fact that your lifestyles and perspectives differ, you can still be friends. In fact, if your bond is deep, it's important to nourish your friendship and hang in there. Your non-Christian friend is more likely to listen to you one day than to someone who doesn't have so much love invested in her. Studies show most individuals who come to Christ as adults do so through the influence of a good friend.

2. Because of your differences, your friendship may experience more friction—so rely on prayer, love, and tact to ease you over the bumps. When we moved to Nebraska, I became friends with a non-Christian neighbor. She and her husband invited us to an R-rated movie. Situations like this can put you between a rock and a hard place: If you make a big issue of refusing, the hurt you inflict may end the friendship and your chance to tell your friend about Christ; if you go, you may compromise your witness. I think it's wise to refuse but to keep the refusal light and offer an alternative.

3. Part of your love for your non-Christian friend should involve praying for her and sharing your faith. If you never talk about Christ, you're like the doctor who has a cure for a patient's terminal disease but simply fluffs her pillows and lets her die. Lori had been friends with her non-Christian neighbor for five years, yet never shared her faith. When she finally gathered her courage, she went over to see her neighbor and said, "Samantha, you are my best friend—and I want so much to know you will be in heaven. Could I share with you how the Bible says you can be sure of going to heaven?" Lori led Samantha to the Lord that day.

Author Paul Little once compared witnessing to watching television: You need both the picture and the sound. If your friend sees the picture with no sound, she won't know what's going on.

4. Go easy on the peripheral issues. Trying to change a friend's lifestyle when she doesn't have Christ is like putting the cart before the horse. As a non-Christian begins to trust you, she is the one who is likely to initiate discussions about lifestyle issues the Lord is convicting her of. Before I came to Christ, I said to the woman who eventually led me to Him: "Sally, Steve and I are planning to build an extravagant house overlooking the Pacific Ocean when he's done with medical school. Do you think if we gave our lives to Christ, God would ask us to give that up?"

Sally wisely responded: "I think so, because God is a jealous God and He doesn't want any other gods before Him. That house seems to be first in your hearts." Sally did not initiate conversations about my lifestyle, she initiated conversations about Jesus Christ—who He is and why He came. Then she let His Spirit do the convicting.

5. *While friendships with non-Christians are different, they are to be valued.* When I'm with my non-Christian friends, I miss being able to pray together, study the Word together, or worship together. But there are many other interests you can share with non-Christians.

Though your friends may not have put their trust in Christ, don't be blinded to their wonderful, God-given qualities. Hilary works at a juvenile detention center, affirming rejected kids. She is caring, loving, and candid. If she ever does give her life to Christ, she will be a powerful servant. I am enriched by my friendship with Hilary and other non-Christians, and I pray that through our friendship they one day may know the Christ who has turned my life around.

—From *Today's Christian Woman* (March/April 1992)

4

How Do I Make Time for Friends?

—Stormie Omartian

LATELY, I'VE LEARNED just how important it is to invest time in my friendships. I was coming down to the deadline on my book *A Step in the Right Direction* (Thomas Nelson), and that meant for about six months the only people getting my attention were my husband and my children. I said to my friends, "I have to put everything on hold for now so please don't judge me on how good a friend I am until this is all over."

My friends were understanding, but to my surprise when I finished the book I felt empty. In terms of friendship, I was like a bucket with a slow leak that had drained dry. I knew I had to take action. As soon as the manuscript was on its way to the publisher, I blocked off a number of days to do something special with each friend I felt I had "neglected." Those turned out to be ten wonderful days, full of happy memories for both my friends and me.

A few friendships needed repair. These friends, not being writers and unable to relate to how demanding a deadline can be, started to wonder, "Can someone really be that busy?" Doubt began to grow in their hearts as they questioned if I really cared about them. Fortunately, I convinced them otherwise, and the friendships were restored. But in the process I learned that it's vital to make time for our friends for two reasons: Friendships strengthen and fulfill us, and if they are not nurtured they die on the vine.

In our modern society, it seems we have stepped on a treadmill that keeps us going a million miles an hour—all the time. I constantly battle being too busy and wonder, "Where can I cut back?"

Part of our problem is the fact we have too many opportunities at our fingertips. We can be involved in so many different activities. So can our kids, which means we're busy carting them here and there. As a result, it can take major effort to get together with a friend. And often in the busyness of life, time for friendship gets pushed to the wayside—we see it as another pull on our time.

TIMING IS EVERYTHING

How much time we can give to a friend often depends on the season of life we're in. It's easier for me at this stage in life to cultivate friendships than it was in my early parenting years with four children under age five. Back then my friends had to be those women who were in the same milieu. I needed friendships as a young mother but often I was too consumed with what I was doing to do much knowing or remembering.

—Colleen

I've learned though, making time for friends has just the opposite effect. In a truly good friendship you aren't depleted but instead built up from the time you spend together. I know from experience that I can't minister to others unless I have the support and prayers of my friends. The time we invest in friendship is so important. But just how do we go about making time for friends despite a packed schedule?

Partners in Prayer

One approach for making time for friends that has worked well for me is to make my closest friends my prayer partners and my prayer partners my closest friends. For years, I've met weekly with a prayer group of six or seven women from our church. While the members have changed over the years, in every group a deep bond has developed between each one of us. We've made a commitment to get together at a set time to share and pray in-depth, and it's a time commitment we take seriously and aren't likely to break. Believe me, you never forget a friend's face as she shares her pain and you pray for her. You have a place in your heart for her the rest of your life.

Not too long ago, the son of a woman in my prayer group was having some serious problems. One morning I got up to pray for him, and in the process I started to sob. I prayed as though I was interceding for his life. When I shared my experience with my friend, she was overwhelmed that I would pray for her son that way. It was this God-given concern for her son that morning that touched her more than anything else I could ever have done and has made us such close friends.

Praying for one another on a regular basis forms a friendship bond that's deeper than any other. Hands down, one of the best ways to establish a strong friendship is to make your friend your prayer partner and set aside a certain time each week to meet for prayer. In prayer you will soon open up your souls and share at a level you might not with someone you only meet for lunch.

Double Up

I am constantly juggling how much time I can give to friendships and still keep my husband and children happy. While I know time for friendship is necessary, fitting it in isn't always easy. What has worked for me is to integrate my time with friends into my lifestyle. Essentially, I double up on activities so I'm maintaining my family's needs while still making time for friends.

For instance, my friend Deborah has a daughter and son who are the same age as my daughter and son and who go to the same schools. We also attend the same church, so our paths often cross both at school and church events. Beyond that, we are also in the same prayer group, so again our paths cross.

I also have another friend, Priscilla, who has a daughter the same age as mine. Whenever a movie comes out that the girls would enjoy, we take them. This gives my friend and me time to talk on the drive to the theater, while we munch our popcorn before the movie starts, and then on the drive home. The girls keep one another occupied, and my friend and I have plenty of time together.

Another friend, Pamela, has a husband who often works late, as mine does. Her children are grown, so I sometimes invite her to join me and my children for dinner. Afterward, we have a chance to chat one-on-one. With a little creative thinking you can easily find the time for friends by working them into your lifestyle.

Be Realistic

Of all my friends, there is only a small handful—my prayer group—to whom I am closest and am able to make the most time for. As much as I'd like to have a deep friendship with everyone I call a friend, it just isn't possible—I simply don't have the time.

When time is limited, it helps to focus your friendships. I know I can maintain regular contact with the six women in my prayer group. Outside of this group are friends that I meet occasionally—say for lunch a few times a year. I make the effort to touch base with them enough so I can maintain our friendship and see how each is doing. While the contact is brief and not as frequent as with close friends, it is still rewarding. We care about each other and are interested in each other's lives, but we know that it's not the kind of relationship that requires getting together every week.

I'm fortunate that my husband likes to spend time with his friends and can understand why I need time with mine. But not all husbands are that understanding. I know some husbands get irritated if their wives are on the phone all the time or seem to spend a lot of time with their friends. If that's the case, it helps to set up some kind of schedule such as a particular night each week or a couple times a month to spend with friends. This way, the time you spend with friends will be viewed by your husband as having a definite beginning and end, and he will still feel like a priority in your life.

My morning phone calls to Diane used to irritate my husband. I didn't think I was on the phone a lot, except that when I was on the phone it was early in the morning and Michael was home. To him it appeared I was *always* talking to Diane. Finally, I explained to him, "I'm not going to be on the phone with her every single day, hour after hour. I just want to pray with her for half an hour three times a week." Michael's irritation ceased once I explained what I was doing, and he knew my calls had a beginning and an end.

WHO COMES FIRST?

A woman once shared with me the fact she couldn't understand why her husband so resented her friendships. As I asked her more about her friendships it became quite clear that her friends took top priority over her relationship with her husband. As she told me all the wonderful things she did with her friends, I didn't see how she possibly had time for her husband. This woman had allowed her time with friends to violate other relationships— namely her marriage.

—Ruth

Know What Your Friends Expect

It helps to periodically look at your friendships and see if you're happy with the amount of time you're investing in them. If I don't do this I know the couple I've been meaning to invite over will never get invited. Keeping myself accountable this way makes me take action on my words.

At times, I wish I was more organized about my friendships. I'd like to keep some kind of informal record about whom I've spent time with and when because I don't always realize how much time has passed since I last talked with a certain friend. While I haven't found a way to be this organized yet, I know it would help me be a better friend.

Friendships must be nurtured if they are to last. It's easy to lose contact with people and soon you don't know what is happening in their lives. If enough time goes by without even a call, a gap can develop between you that widens until the friendship withers from neglect.

I encourage every woman to take her friendships before the Lord and say, "Lord, show me what I should be doing to honor this friendship and help me find the time to do it."

Although I'm not fond of lengthy phone conversations, I'm finding there are a few friends who feel very hurt if I don't extend myself to call them. I spend time with friends on the phone, even though it's not my favorite thing to do, because it's an act of caring.

Making time for friendship is important because the time you spend with a friend enriches you as a person. I know those contacts with my closest friends keep me alive, sharp, and full of fresh ideas. I have a variety of close friends and each brings something different to my life—something special. Despite our busy lives, we can't afford to fall into the excuse of "I don't have the time for friends." We have a ministry to them, and they have a ministry to us. And besides, experience has proven to me that we will have time for what we want to have time for.

Make It Happen

1. If time is short, look for those activities that allow you to combine time for friends. Be creative! Consider serving on the food committee at church with a friend. As you pack food baskets and deliver them, you'll have time to share in conversation. If you're trying to work exercise into your daily routine, ask a friend to walk with you. It helps the miles go faster when you're talking.

2. If your contact with friends seem a little haphazard, then each time you make a contact with a friend—

phone call, lunch, or walk—make a note of it in your calendar. Then at a glance, you'll know what friends need to be contacted next. And, if you want, even make a note of what's happening in that friend's life so when you do talk again you can remember where your conversation left off.

3. Invest the most time in that handful of friendships that mean the most to you. Remember, you can only have a small number of close friendships. Don't spread yourself too thin because if you do you'll end up frustrated. Set limits on how much time you can reasonably expect to spend on friendships after considering your other priorities.

4. On a piece of paper make four columns. Title the columns: (1) close friends; (2) good friends; (3) casual friends, and (4) budding friendships. Review all of your friendships and place each friend under the appropriate category. Now, look over your list and reflect on how you are spending your time. Are there some names you'd like to see moved from the casual friends to the close friends category? Are you willing to invest more time for that to happen? Use the insights you've gained from this exercise to help you determine where to best use your time.

Circle of Friends
Jan Johnson with Jane J. Struck

The more women I talk to, the more I discover an undercurrent of pain and confusion about church friendships. A surprising number of Christian women experience loneliness and frustration because they haven't found vital relationships that meet their social and spiritual needs in the place they most expect fellowship. Whether we're new to the church, too burned out from the demands on our time and energy, or find it difficult to be transparent with others, the truth of the matter is, these friendships often don't just happen. Here are some practical ways to help you change from being a face in the crowd on Sunday mornings to a friend.

Look for other women who need friends. Chances are, if you're feeling lonely in church, there are several other women who feel the same way you do. If you take a look beyond your own needs and expectations, you'll often find others who also are hoping someone will reach out to *them.*

My pastor suggested a "three-minute rule" one Sunday that has helped me do just that. The "three-minute rule" is this: for the first three minutes before and after a church service, make it a point to talk to someone you don't know and make her feel welcome. This "rule" has forced me to be active instead of passive in the friendship process. I gather my courage, take a deep breath, and greet people. As I get into conversations with them, I keep my "friendship antenna" out. Is this person someone I'd like to know better? Is this a hurting woman who needs a friend?

Be transparent. Even if we dress up for church, that doesn't mean we have to dress up our attitudes and pretend we have no struggles. I would never have made one of my friends if I hadn't blundered ahead and told her that I felt lonely. Transparency is the key to friendship. To be a friend, we have to be honest about who we are and what we're feeling.

Develop a strategy. "There are lots of interesting people in my church," a woman recently told me. "But I don't feel comfortable just walking up to them and saying, 'Could I be your friend? I'd like to get to know you.' "

It *can* be intimidating to seek out someone and try to develop a friendship—we're all worried about the possibility of rejection. Develop a strategy *you* feel comfortable with to break the ice with some church women you think you might like to get to know. Sarah, a fairly new member of a large Sunday school class, decided to call and invite a different woman over for coffee or lunch at her home every other week or so. "It was much easier for me to invite these women over the phone than at church," she explains. "And I found it easier to be open and friendly in a one-on-one situation in my own home, rather than during the church coffee hours where everyone tends to congregate into little groups. Sometimes a friendship clicked, sometimes it didn't—but I'm working at it."

Look for commonalities. Listen carefully in conversations for possible "friendship magnets." Similar hobbies and interests, such as aerobics or choir, draw women together.

Having children the same age drew Lesly and me together. Her son invited mine over to play, and when I brought him, she invited me to come in for coffee. We often share ideas and give each other moral support since our kids are growing through similar stages.

Volunteer to serve. One powerful commonality is serving side-by-side with someone. "I didn't know anyone in our large church," Jeanne tells me, "but I felt I needed to get involved and help in a homeless shelter our church operates. A wonderful by-product of serving the Lord is the friendships I'm forming with women who are similarly involved. I wasn't in it for the friendships—but they've happened."

Set realistic expectations for friendship. "I always struggle with wanting to be 'popular,' even in church," says Cindy, a co-worker. "But with my schedule and energy level, it's just not realistic for me to expect to have a dozen church friends. I have to pinch myself sometimes and say, *Get real. What do you really want, and what can you handle?*'

Friends can come into our lives through many different contacts. But the encouragement and support we gain from fellowship with people who share our faith are invaluable. Making friends at church involves a risk, a faith walk, if you will. We step out, speak to someone, and share ourselves. But even as we take that risk, we can be confident in knowing God is aware of *all* our needs—even for Christian friends—and be confident in His provision.

—From *Today's Christian Woman (January/February 1992)*

5

What Are Some Principles I Need to Keep in Mind As I Develop Friendships With the Opposite Sex?

—Colleen Evans

AUTHOR KAREN MAINS once wrote, "Holy friendship between men and women is an eschatological sign of what God intends creation to be on that day when profound restoration finally comes." I agree with her and I believe godly male/female friendships are good and meant to be. That said, friendships with men can be tricky. It takes discernment to know and maintain the boundaries of friendship with a man.

Some women, and married women in particular, feel it's impossible and unwise to have male friends. While this perspective may be right for some, in my experience such a narrow view causes us to miss out on some of life's most enriching relationships. God created us male and female not simply for marriage and procreation—if that were the case then the numbers would come out exactly right and everyone would have a mate. I believe God created us male and female to complement one another in society through healthy, godly friendships, as well. Men and women need each other in terms of our particular gifts—there are definite qualities women can bring to men and, likewise, men can bring to women. And while I hesitate to generalize on the specifics of these attributes, it is fair to say there is a distinct male perspective and female perspective on life.

I serve on several boards of directors for Christian organizations. When I attend board meetings, I see the variety of give-and-take between men and women— each adds something to the others' thinking processes. And that give-and-take, whether it happens in the church or the workplace, affirms in my mind the fact that men and women are meant to be friends and work side by side in society—and in the Church—in a healthy and complementary manner.

The Bible points to this natural friendship between men and women. Throughout the New Testament the Scriptures talk about brothers and sisters in relationship—men and women as friends, co-laborers in Christ. Jesus was a terrific model of male/female friendship by the way He anointed such relationships. He befriended women like Mary and Martha. He went to their home, perhaps took off His sandals, and had a glass of pomegranate juice with them. He engaged them in serious theological discussion. They were true brothers and sisters.

Jesus astonished people when He accepted women as intellectual/spiritual equals. I don't think we can truly grasp how radical Jesus' behavior was until we realize that in His day a good religious Jewish man simply *didn't* acknowledge women as equals—let alone a Samaritan woman or a woman of the streets. Yet Jesus did just that and in His actions showed respect for women as people. Jesus showed us that friendships between men and women can be a very rich part of life.

However, there are differences between opposite-sex friendships and same-sex friendships that we can't ignore if we want our friendships with men to be godly, healthy relationships.

Know Yourself

If you're married, one of the first guidelines is to realize that your marriage is absolutely primary. I love my husband. I respect him. He is my number-one human priority. No male/female friendships should ever infringe upon the marriage relationship in terms of time, energy, or intimacy. Likewise, if you're single, no relationship should detract from your devotion to Christ. To prevent that friendship from encroaching on your marriage or your spiritual life, you need to be aware of your "Achilles' heel"—that small yet mortal weakness we each have. In other words, in what area are you vulnerable when it comes to relationships?

Louie and I know a man whose "Achilles' heel" is his enormous need to be fawned over. A powerful business entrepreneur, he is used to being the focus of attention. He has a wonderful wife, but she is quiet by nature and isn't openly affectionate. As a result, this man has been involved in mental and physical infidelity throughout his marriage because his need to be flattered isn't met by his wife. If he was aware of his inordinate need for affirmation he might be more careful in his friendships with women and where they lead. And, he could begin to see the very real ways in which his wife supports and affirms him.

As you develop friendships with the opposite sex, be aware of your needs and aware of the fact that it's tempting to have those needs filled outside the home. I know some lively, talkative women who are frustrated because they are married to quiet men—what author David Augsburger calls the "babbling brook/dead sea" syndrome. While their spouses may never fulfill their needs for verbal sharing, these women at least owe it to their husbands to express their needs and desires for more communication and commit to work on that aspect of their relationship rather than find another man who will listen to them and fill this basic need.

———— ⁊ ————

While basic intimate needs should be met *within* the marriage there are many needs that can be met by an opposite-sex friend that are perfectly appropriate. For instance, I love to be involved in and wrestle with issues—politics, the world, and the plight of our inner-cities. Louie does too, but because of his call to *other* aspects of ministry he cannot share my level of involvement in these things. So during our life together, I have always had a circle of friends, both male and female, with whom I share these deep-hearted interests. Because my need is not based on an intimate, emotional longing, but rather on a desire to share a God-designed part of my life, there is nothing wrong with including men in that circle of friends who share my interests. Likewise, Louie has sisters who are colleagues in ministry with whom he shares warm affection and trust. These opposite-sex friends enrich our life, and our marriage, *but they exist always and only within the context of fidelity!*

Make a Mental Note

For Christian couples, the matter of fidelity is settled. But fidelity is not just physical—it's mental as well. We cannot keep our friendships with men purely platonic if we are engaging in inappropriate fantasies of them. I firmly believe that physical infidelity starts in your mind—not in your erogenous zones, but right between your ears! If we are going to enjoy friendships with men, we need to commit ourselves to total fidelity—body and mind. If your thinking begins to deteriorate and you catch yourself entertaining less than pure thoughts of your friend, you need to take action immediately. Better to stop a rolling stone before it gains momentum! Some people would say it's unhealthy to repress thoughts from the mind. But to me, making a conscious choice to be faithful with your mind and heart as well as your body is the far healthier choice. We need to put extra emphasis on mental fidelity if we're going to have friends of the opposite sex. And we have to make it transparently clear to our male friends by our attitude, actions, and demeanor that anything beyond friendship is simply not an option. If you find someone who has difficulty adhering to these kinds of boundaries and he pushes for something beyond friendship—if the line is at all fuzzy—then you need to call off the friendship. Remember your devotion to Christ and your marriage are primary. It's not worth the risk of continuing the friendship.

THIS WAY OUT

If a friendship with the opposite sex makes you discontent with your spouse, you need to post a "danger zone" sign and quickly make your exit.

—Ruth

Husbands and wives need to be very honest with each other and themselves if they see danger in an opposite-sex friendship. No secrets allowed. Louie and I have been married over forty years and only on the rarest occasion have I ever felt the need to say to Louie, "Honey, watch out for that one! I don't think that friend has the same thing in mind as you do. She's a lovely woman, but I don't think she understands what it means when you say, 'You're my sister in the Lord.'"

As a pastor, Louie has done thousands of hours of counseling, and in a few cases it did end up that the woman he was counseling was fantasizing about him. But thankfully, Louie has a good warning system, wise pastoral procedures, and, most of all, a pure heart! Even so, once or twice, sensing he had missed a clue, I have talked to him about a concern. I really feel that when a spouse is uneasy in this area, he or she needs to speak up *immediately* and prevent any silent anxieties from building. Talk about it even at the risk of your spouse thinking you are jealous. Many couples make a mistake by *not* talking about their concerns because they don't want to come across as being petty. But if your marriage is primary, you'll take that risk.

Focus

I've found one of the best guidelines for male/female friendships is the need for the friendship to have a focus. By focus I mean your friendship takes place within the setting of a certain activity. That focus might be a group Bible study, a committee at church, projects, or work. As I've said, most of my male friends are from our covenant group, colleagues from the boards I serve on, or from the ministries I'm involved in.

Just this morning, I was at a conference where the focus of the friendship between myself and some male friends was our mutual interest in the renewal of the church. When we first meet, we'll naturally log in about what's going on in our world—if married—we check on how our spouses and families are doing, but then the focus of our time together is our work. Our work brings us together, gives us a focus, and in the process sets up boundaries for our friendship.

One woman I know is very good friends with a male colleague. Even though they enjoy working together and make a good team, she knows that a dinner out with this man without her husband is out of the question. Such a dinner would take the friendship out of focus. Since her husband doesn't know this man well, she told me, "I have to keep the boundaries of our friendship clear and the boundary is work." She keeps the focus of their friendship sharp.

Context

Besides having a focus to the friendship, there needs to be a context as well. For me, one of my closest male friendships has occurred within the context of a couple friendship. Louie and I are very close to Mary Jane and John, friends from our Washington days. Mary Jane and Louie were on the same church staff in Washington for years and were colleagues in ministry. The time they spent together was focused on their work. John and I, on the other hand, led an adult nurture class called "The Wrestlers" (wrestling with issues from a biblical perspective) for ten years. It was great fun and grew into a wonderful ministry in the church. John was a member of Congress, and later was appointed director of the Peace Corps. His interest is the world and so is mine. Our interests are so alike—the world, ministry to the poor, and the application of biblical truth to contemporary life—and *these* interests are the focus of our friendship. And yet, Louie and John are great friends. Mary Jane and I are true covenant sisters. Our love and friendship goes in every direction. When we get together for a day, Mary Jane and I go out and have coffee and talk about the interests we share, which are many. Then, later in the day she and Louie get together and talk psychology and ministry while John and I talk Africa. The context of my brother/sister relationship with John is within our couple friendship. I don't think of John without thinking of Mary Jane. John doesn't think about me apart from Louie. And in this context, John and I can be true friends.

Not long ago, Louie and I were having dinner with our Pakistani neighbor friends. In our discussion that evening, the husband shared that in his culture once a man marries a woman, all of his brothers and his best friends call his wife "sister." They become like a close family. A friendship now exists within the context of a large family.

Our friendships with men should not take place in isolation, but rather as part of a larger context of friendships. I could not be such a buddy with my brother John if he didn't know and love Louie and if I didn't know and love Mary Jane. We could be friends in our focused areas of interest, but our friendship could not have developed into a true brother/sister relationship without the parameters of our couple friendship.

NOT WORTH THE RISK

After I was married, I decided out of respect for my husband I would not have a close friendship with a male. To have such a friend would require I spend time alone with that person and there is a great danger in that. All it takes is one moment of thinking, "This man understands me better and treats me nicer than my husband," and you're in trouble. No friendship is worth the risk of jeopardizing your marriage—no matter how slight the possibility may seem.

—Stormie

Male/female friendships can be challenging, but they are possible if you proceed with caution. If you do, then you are likely to have rewarding, healthy friendships with members of the opposite sex. Male/female friendships are important because women help men understand and broaden their view of women and vice versa. Such friendships help us break down the stereotypes we often have of the opposite sex. The more men you have as friends the more you hesitate to categorize and say, "Men do this," or "All men are like that." Men are different just as women are different. Because of Louie and the male friends I have, I now know that some men are highly intuitive and expressive. My husband is multi-gifted—very mechanically inclined and strong, but not all men are the same as Louie. Without my male friends, it would be easy to generalize and judge every man against Louie.

As women, we make up one half of humanity. We need to relate to the other half. I don't think it is healthy—or in line with God's design for our lives—to think that we can only relate to our own sex. Yet because we are physical and emotional creatures, as we develop opposite-sex friendships we need to have certain holy guidelines in place. And once those are in place, then we open up the opportunity for many rich and rewarding relationships.

Make It Happen

1. Look at your friendships with men. Are they within the guidelines Colleen spoke of? Do they have a focus and a context? Do they allow for your marriage to stay as your number-one priority? If your friendship falls short of these guidelines, then take steps today to build it into a healthy, godly relationship.

2. What is your "Achilles' heel"? What need in your life drives you and often undermines you? Is it the need to be the center of attention, to feel cherished, or to have constant affirmation? Be honest with yourself. Probe a close friend or your spouse about what they see in you as a weakness. Don't be discouraged over your weakness, but rather be aware of it and how it affects your choice of friends and your behavior. While God didn't make us perfect, He did provide us with a perfect Savior who understands and supports us in our weaknesses.

3. Look for opportunities within your contacts for possible friendships with men. Rather than shy away from potential friendships, look at them as an oppor-

tunity to understand men better. The knowledge you gain can help in all areas of your life as well as reinforce the truth that God created each one of us with specific gifts, talents, and temperaments to do the work of His kingdom.

PART TWO

Breaking Down the Barriers to Friendship

HUNDREDS OF BARRIERS exist to friendship. The time and energy alone that a friendship requires sometimes prove to be the biggest obstacles to a friendship's growth. But what happens when we do go that extra mile in a friendship? When we do break down what seems like an impenetrable barrier? Ruth Senter found out one day.

As she and her husband, Mark, drove through a small town in Alabama where she'd lived in her early childhood, Ruth decided to look up Susie, a friend Ruth hadn't seen in more than seventeen years. Much to Ruth's surprise, one phone call later, she and Susie were reunited. Ruth had called Susie's mother from the very drugstore Susie's husband owned.

The two connected and the friendship was reestablished. That was twenty-four years ago, and as Ruth looks back today she realizes, "My friendship with Susie is one of the most precious friendships I have—she's my connection to my childhood—she's gold. And yet I almost missed the chance because Mark and I were tired, we needed to keep going, and the likelihood of Susie still living in that town seemed so remote."

"My life is richer thanks to my friendship with Susie," admits Ruth. When we take the chance, when we dare to break down the barriers to friendship, we, too, can open our lives to a richness that only friends can bring.

In the following chapters, Colleen, Stormie, and

Ruth explore the obstacles that can undermine friendship, such as possessiveness, distance, or jealousy, and then offer practical insights on how we can move beyond these obstacles.

6

How Can I Tell If a Friendship Is Unhealthy?

—Ruth Senter

MY LIFE IS RICH today with friendships from all seasons of my life—childhood (my friend from first and second grade and I still correspond and get together even though years and miles separate us), high school, college, and adulthood. As valuable and meaningful as life-long friendships are to me, I've lived long enough to realize some friendships don't last a lifetime. Some come and go with the season. However, I firmly believe in Ecclesiastes 3, "There is a time for everything, and a season for every activity under heaven. . . . There is a time to embrace and a time to refrain" (vss. 1, 5). Although these words were written in reference to life in general, they can be applied to friendships as well.

You and I are never the same person twice—even from day to day. We are neither static nor predictable. Some changes in us are minimal and barely affect our friendships. At other times, though, the changes are so significant that they can take us or our friend down a completely different road and forever change the chemistry between us. Hopefully, our friendships will move toward the positive, but sometimes, because of the ever-changing nature of people and our lives, friendships can deteriorate into unhealthy relationships. How, then, can we know if it is time to embrace a friendship, or time to let go?

Over the years, I've discovered several traits that tend to point to an unhealthy friendship. Though the traits vary, the common denominator in all unhealthy friendships is need. When one person seeks out the friendship of another based on what she needs or what she can get out of the relationship, this friendship is destined for unhappiness.

Solve My Problems, Please

When friends look to you to solve their problems and they become dependent on you, your friendship is need-driven. For instance, when my husband, Mark, and I were in youth ministry I became friends with one girl—a real likable kid. Over time, though, I noticed our conversations would inevitably focus on her mother and her home situation. I tried to give constructive advice, but we never got anywhere. This theme repeated itself week after week. Finally I said, "I don't want you to call me again until you tell your mother exactly what you've told me." When she called several days later, the first thing I asked was, "Have you talked to your mother?"

"No," she said, "but let me tell you just one more thing."

"Our agreement was you need to talk to your mother about the situation," I reminded her.

It soon became evident that my friend would rather talk about her problems than solve them. When she continually failed to act on my suggestions, I knew there was a problem. It was hard for me to stand firm but I knew the continued pattern in our friendship wasn't doing her any good.

When someone would rather talk to me about her problems than seek solutions, that's good evidence of an unbalanced need in a friendship. It was obvious my friend didn't really want her problems solved—she got more attention when she complained about her problems.

If you think you're in a similar situation, ask yourself a few simple questions. "Who does most of the talking in this relationship? Does my friend ever do anything with my advice? Whose problems are we genuinely trying to solve or trying to work through?" If it's always the other person, that's a good hint the friendship lacks balance.

Another indicator of a needy friend who is becoming too dependent on you is when a friend needs to talk with you urgently and frequently and always about her problems. I realized this was happening with one friend when she began every phone call with, "I have to talk to you." There was a continual sense of urgency in her voice, and I sensed that for her talking to me was like taking a pill.

It's not only how a friend says things to you, it's what she's saying as well. In a friendship with a dependent person I would hear statements like, "You're the only one who understands." Now, right away that raises my anxiety level. I begin to feel like this person is drowning and I'm the only person who can save her. If I don't come up with a diagnosis and a solution, this person's going to get pulled under. That's too much responsibility for any one person. And while we all have a choice whether to accept this kind of responsibility or not, it's still an unfair load to dump on one friend.

A friend who depends on you too much for her emotional support often has a victim orientation to life and frequently says things like, "Just my luck. Nothing ever goes right for me." It's important to clarify the difference between a person in need and a needy person. A person in need is basically an emotionally healthy person who happens to be going through a tough time and needs you to help her regain perspective. This person is honestly seeking solutions and is willing to draw up plans to move toward those solutions. A needy person continually talks about her problems yet never takes steps toward resolving them. She is always ready with an excuse if counseling is suggested. She refuses to be held accountable. After all, it's much easier to go through life having everyone think, *Poor Sally, she's had such a hard time* and then making allowances for her.

Believe it or not, even having the same friend call you all the time asking you to pray for her can be an indication of a needy friend, especially when she never seems to want to do anything about her particular problem or need. Ask yourself, "Is my friend always on my prayer request list and never on my praise list? It's affirming to have someone pray for us but it can also be an attention-getter. Sadly, there are people who love being prayer requests rather than being answers to prayer.

———— ✐ ————

If you don't see your friend taking some positive steps in her life then you might want to consider lessening your helper role. When Jesus dealt with people, He never did for them what He thought they should do for themselves. He expected a degree of personal responsibility. When God deals with us He doesn't make our choices for us. He doesn't unroll the blueprint and say, "Take step A, then B, and then C." Rather, He gives us the broad strokes. He gives us the principles and says, "Now, you work it out in a Christlike, godly manner."

In the same way, why should we feel as though we need to draw a map for a friend and assure her if she'll just follow this dotted line everything will be okay? One reason we end up in this type of unhealthy friendship is because it feels good to be in charge—to be in control of someone else's life. It can be very satisfying to our ego, and for that reason we need to look carefully at whether our role of the helper is breeding an unhealthy dependence on us.

If you see your friendship moving toward unhealthy dependency ask yourself, "Am I developing a savior complex?" By that I mean, are you starting to think, "I'm the only one who can save her." That is a dangerous reason to help someone. As Christians, we do not meet another's need as a way of meeting a need in ourselves. We meet other's needs as a natural overflow of God's love in us.

There are benefits to helping someone—you can see that person blossom and move beyond their hurt. But if you ask yourself, "Why am I doing this?" and realize you're doing it because you desperately need to be needed, then you should pull back from the friendship.

The source of the greatest emotional drains in my life aren't the major crises, but little leaks. An unhealthy friendship can be one of those "little leaks." Our brain can creatively deal with only so many problems at a time. And if you have an overload on a particular friend's problems, then often there's nothing left for solving the daily problems you face. It's hard to be consistent in disciplining a child who has written on the living room wall when you are forever listening on the phone to a friend rattling on about her problems.

A friendship is moving toward unhealthy territory when an unequal amount of give-and-take exists. For instance, do you continually feel you must appease a friend and take the blame for whatever happens in the friendship? Do you hear yourself making statements like, "I should have called you, but . . ." or "I should have invited you, but . . ."? Do you often feel you are on the defensive and solely responsible for the maintenance of the relationship? Ask yourself, "Is this friendship a two-way investment? Am I receiving as much from this relationship as I am giving?" If not, it needs some adjustment and you need to realize you're taking on far more responsibility for a friendship than you should.

NO ROOM FOR GUILT

A good friend won't lay expectations on me that make me feel guilty nor should I do this to her. Rather, a friend should make me feel as though she enjoys being with me and vice versa. A good, healthy friendship should be one that has an attitude of joy.

—Colleen

I Want to Be Like You

Another unhealthy need that motivates a friendship is a person's desire to be close to you because of your position, status, or money. When my husband was on the pastoral staff of a church, I once felt like someone was more interested in getting the scoop on what was happening in the church than she was in what was going on in my life. Maybe she wanted to be close to the center of information, and since my husband was on staff she assumed I knew what he knew. Fortunately, I soon realized this was not a healthy base for a friendship and was able to discourage any further development.

I once went to lunch with a woman who had a great deal of money and influence in the community. We started talking about friendships. She shared with me that she had been hurt a number of times because she felt her "friends" weren't as interested in who she was as they were in her position in the community. It wasn't long before she started to feel used. It was evident to her that certain friends liked their association with her because of the fringe benefits her money brought, like an invitation to the country club or a black-tie dinner. Relationships based solely on this kind of need are usually very short-lived and, for both parties, such friendships are neither healthy nor satisfying.

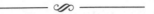

Closely related to the need to associate with someone because of their position or money is the need to belong to a particular group. Belonging is a normal need, but one that can cause us to form friendships for the wrong reason. At one time or another, I'm sure we've all felt like the outsider and wanted desperately to be part of the inner circle. As a result, we work too hard to make the friendship happen.

I've learned to ask myself some questions to help keep my motives for a friendship in line. "Am I working too hard to make this happen? Do I always want to be part of what she does with her group? Do I try too hard to be friends with all her friends?" One of the principles I've found freeing is that if I have to work too hard to open the door, it may be a door I shouldn't go through.

And likewise, we need to evaluate those who are extending themselves to us in friendship. While we can't know another person's motives for certain, we can look for clues. Does the other person seem more focused on your group than on you? If every time you're talking with your friend, she's looking around the room to see who else is there or you sense your words are falling on deaf ears, you might need to ask yourself if this person is really interested in you or only in what you can do for her. Chances are if you pursue a relationship based on someone's need to belong it will not be a healthy, mutually rewarding friendship.

I Have to Have Somebody

Another need that can lead to an unhealthy friendship is insecurity. People can be so desperate for a friend—they want a friend for the sake of having a friend. I remember kids in high school whose friendships were born out of insecurities or loneliness. The trademark of those friendships was possessiveness and jealousy on the part of one person in the relationship.

As a young girl, one of my friendships took on this sense of possessiveness, although at the time I didn't realize why my friend behaved as she did. Whenever I talked to my friend about another friend, she would either become very quiet, or put down the friend I mentioned. After awhile, I realized I was her only friend and when you have only one friend you hang on tight.

It's important to go into a friendship with your eyes wide open. One way to do so is to look at the other relationships a person has cultivated. If you don't see her working on other relationships or she doesn't appear to have other friends, enter such a friendship cautiously. Look for reasons why this person has no other friends.

If you do choose to get involved, then do so with the goal of helping this person use your friendship as a stepping stone to opening herself up to other people. If you can model for her a healthy relationship (given there are enough characteristics in the friendship that make it the kind of relationship you want to invest time in), then you have the potential to help her understand all that friendship can be.

Time to Assess the Friendship

Sometimes, even as wonderful and right as a friendship seems, it can still use an occasional checkup. And while it's not a good idea to reduce our friendships to some kind of species to be put under a microscope, there is something to be said for periodically assessing our friendships to determine if they are healthy. Surprisingly, this assessment doesn't stifle a friendship, but instead, I've discovered, it provides the freedom to let the relationship go where it may.

Assessing friendships is much like taking a periodic

personal inventory of my life. If I never stop to consider whether I'm going down the right road in life, I will never know if I'm lost. Once a year I try to get away by myself and take an informal assessment of my relationships as well as of my spiritual life and my emotional and physical health.

I try to look for any blind spots in my friendships. For instance, I know how easy it is to fall into the trap of letting others do all the giving in a friendship. Last year, as I was thinking over my friendships, I realized I was getting very lazy in my letter-writing to friends who lived far away. They were doing more of the six-page letters where they told me not only what was happening in their lives but how they were feeling about it. Or they were suggesting the books I should read or giving me the quotes to think about. I was taking all this in and it was wonderful. And while I was giving to other people, I wasn't giving back to them.

I'd tend to pick up the phone and give them a quick call here and there, or scribble a quick note. But it struck me that while I was keeping in touch, I wasn't making the sacrifice of taking the time to spell out my thoughts and feelings on paper. As a result, I was convicted that I needed to spend my Sunday afternoons writing letters to my friends. Thanks to my year-end assessment I was able to make some minor adjustments in my friendships.

Bringing Back Equilibrium

Assessing our friendships is one way to keep them moving in a positive direction, but what do we do once we realize a friendship isn't as healthy as it should be? Just how do we handle those friendships that are motivated by unhealthy needs?

What has helped me the most is to look at how Jesus dealt with people. He was the Savior, the helper, the ultimate care-giver. If I want to know how to care for someone and yet maintain a balance, I look at Jesus. He withdrew from people at times—even from crisis situations.

When Lazarus died and Mary and Martha sent an urgent Western Union telegram to Jesus asking Him to catch the next bus for Bethany, Jesus chose not to respond. Was it because He needed two more days of vacation in Jerusalem? No, I think it was because He had the bigger picture in mind.

If you're going to have healthy friendships, you have to be distanced enough from another's needs so you don't lose the bigger picture. If Jesus had come right away, Mary and Martha could not have seen His full glory—namely His raising Lazarus from the dead.

NO ONE IS IMMUNE

It's disillusioning when something goes wrong between you and a friend—especially if that friend is a sister in the Lord. But things can and will go wrong because we're all in the human condition and susceptible to envy or jealousy. We are also a complex web of our past, present, and future. So even though we don't expect problems in a friendship, we shouldn't be surprised when they do happen.

—Stormie

In unhealthy friendships, the principle to remember is to maintain a balance, and sometimes that may even be achieved by withdrawing from a friend for a while if you know the relationship is becoming unhealthy or demanding more than you can possibly give. When I took Jori, our firstborn, in for her immunizations, it was agony to see that needle stick her tender skin. But the thought occurred to me as I sat there in the doctor's office, *Yes, this shot is going to hurt, but it is going to spare Jori from a much greater hurt—namely diseases like tetanus or diphtheria.* Sometimes in friendship I may need to temporarily wound for the long-term good of another person. It is a hard but necessary part of friendship.

———— ✑ ————

In an unhealthy friendship we do what we can to make it healthy, but sometimes we may need to withdraw. We need to keep in mind the need for balance, the fact that our needs must be cared for in the relationship as well. The bigger picture of our emotional health as well as the good of the friend. At times we need to stop protecting the other person. We may need to allow the other person to struggle for a while for the sake of her personal growth.

We need to assess our friendships periodically to make sure they are healthy. We need to recognize that just as we are never the same person, even from moment to moment, our friendships will change too. As true friends, we need to be open to dealing with those changes and look for ways to keep our friendships healthy.

Make It Happen

1. Take a few moments to think about your friends. It might even help to list the names. As you look at each name ask yourself, "Am I giving as much as I'm receiving in this friendship and vice versa? Is the friendship going anywhere—am I growing through this relationship? Do we complement each other and look for ways to build each other up? Am I being honest with this person?" If the answers to these questions are "yes" then you can relax—your friendship is most likely healthy. If a few "nos" were sprinkled in your answers, then it's time to make some adjustments.

2. Know your weak spots—areas that could lead to unhealthy friendships. For instance, do you have a strong need to be needed, to solve others' problems? If so, be aware that you might be unknowingly attracting needy people. While we do need to show care and compassion for others, too many needy friends can become an emotional drain. Balance in friendships—an equal give-and-take—is essential to healthy friendships as well as your own emotional health.

3. Are you so absorbed in the needs and problems of your friend that your ability to concentrate is destroyed? Are other primary relationships in your life suffering as a result? Is your husband only getting part of you? Are you only half-tuned in to your children? Is contact with other friends suffering? Remember, one sign of an unhealthy friendship is when it violates other relationships. If that's happening in your life, then step back from the unhealthy friendship and take a breather.

4. Even though it may hurt, be honest with yourself about your friendships. Be aware that you can be used, as well as use people. From time to time, stop and examine your motives for friendship.

How Healthy Are Your Friendships?
Janis Long Harris

Recently, I talked with several Christian women about how they evaluate their friendships. What kind of friendships build them up? What do they do about friendships that impede their Christian growth? Regardless of how they evaluate a friendship, they all agree evaluation is essential. They also agree that both helpful and unhelpful friendships have distinct characteristics. Here are two notable distinctives and how you can turn a negative situation into a positive one.

Positive friendships help you grow spiritually, intellectually, and emotionally. Negative friendships do the opposite. Consider Connie, who sees sharp contrasts between her friendships with her neighbor and her co-worker. Connie's next-door neighbor is chronically unhappy. Connie finds spending too much time with her neighbor not only drains her but also reinforces behavior she's trying to weed out of her life.

But spending time with her co-worker is another story. "My friendship with her is so positive," says Connie. "We memorize Scripture together. We work on projects together. We work on helping each other find biblical solutions to our problems. I see positive products coming out of our friendship, and that makes it very special."

Positive friendships affirm your best qualities. Negative friendships reinforce your worst. Emily knows she has a tendency to be overly critical of others and she's working on keeping her speech "criticism-free." But she has one friend who brings out her belittling chatter.

"After talking with this friend I'll often think, *I've crossed the border and said some very unflattering things,*" says Emily.

"The problem is, I really like my friend. She's fun."

Emily is struggling with the knowledge that her fun friend is someone who reinforces her weaknesses.

Victoria, on the other hand, says she's grateful for friends who encourage her to greater heights. "Just recently, a friend from church called and said, 'Let's get together every other week and read books about prayer,' " recalls Victoria. "I said, 'I don't have time for that, but my prayer life could use help. If you want to get together by phone and report to each other on our prayer life, count me in.' We did, and it's been helpful to have a friend who holds me accountable for praying."

Shifting Gears

Just because a friendship isn't building you up right now doesn't negate its potential to someday be positive. Often a small dose of gentle confrontation can guide a basically healthy friendship on course.

Sometimes there are subtle ways to make time with a friend more productive. One woman, for example, found a solution to the frustration she felt whenever her neighbor stopped by to drink tea and complain about her marriage. "I look for ways to make our time more constructive," she says. "Sometimes I suggest we go for a walk, so at least we're getting exercise while she's chattering away."

Balancing Act

It's not always possible to achieve a balance of give-and-take within a friendship. That's why balance *among* our friendships is so important. Mary Ann, for example, says she has three kinds of friends: first, those who are ahead of her spiritually, emotionally, and intellectually and therefore challenge her; second, those who are behind her whom she can help; and finally, those who are at her level with whom she can, in her words, "stagger along together."

Mary Ann believes—and I'm convinced she's right—that growth requires friends in all three categories.

When to Pull Back

Paula, a friend at work, suffered from an ever-deepening depression that began to interfere with her productivity. For more than a year I listened to her tearful monologues about personal and professional losses. I tried to encourage her, offer her unconditional acceptance, and give her helpful suggestions. But she slid deeper and deeper into angry melancholy.

Eventually, she started lashing out at me. Realizing my attempts at friendship over the past months had been fruitless, I felt frustrated and fearful her self-defeating attitudes would rub off on me. So I began to pull back from the friendship.

When that inevitable guilt crept in, my husband reminded me that my efforts to help Paula not only hadn't worked, but seemed to have reinforced her self-pity. Although I never dropped Paula as a friend, I retreated significantly from the intensity of our relationship.

I've come to realize there *is* a point when a friendship needs to be evaluated. I've discovered that, having evaluated a friendship and found it wanting, I have to take action: I can find a way to refocus the relationship, or I can pull back. Or, if there's a good reason for continuing it, I can balance the friendship with others that build me up.

I want to make sure my friendships encourage me and that I encourage my friends in return.

—From *Today's Christian Woman* (May/June 1991)

7
How Can I Repair a Broken Friendship?

—Stormie Omartian

FRIENDSHIP IS EXTREMELY important to me, maybe even more so than for most people, because of my childhood. I was raised by a mentally ill mother and was isolated from developing any close friendships during my early years. Because I place such a great value on friends, the breakup of a friendship is very painful to me. About four years ago, a close friendship began to erode. Never had something like this happened to me in my adult life.

Laura* and I had been friends for nearly twenty years. However, when Laura started to become critical of me, our friendship began to show signs of strain. In Laura's eyes, my life seemed to be going well while hers was full of setbacks. Over time, her jealousy led to a sense of bitterness and resentment, and I grew increasingly unable to bear her constant criticism. After nearly two years of growing bitterness, Laura dropped out of my life. To my shock, a close friendship appeared to be over. I was stunned.

---

*Laura is a pseudonym.

Go the Extra Mile

As Christians, we can't be casual about our friendships because, as I mentioned in an earlier chapter, our friendships have eternal consequences. Beyond that, a friend is a gift and a treasure—someone God brings into our lives. We need to nurture our friendships, and sometimes that means going the extra mile.

Because my goal is always to preserve a friendship, I'm usually quick to bear the burden of responsibility when problems surface. A few years ago, there was a misunderstanding between a friend and me. What I said to my friend was wrongly interpreted and as a result her feelings were hurt. When she later told me how much my words hurt her, I apologized for what I said. It would have been tempting to say, "You misinterpreted me and how you feel is really your problem," but instead I said, "I'm sorry if what I said hurt you. I never meant it the way it must have sounded to you. Please forgive me." Her forgiveness of me was more important than my proving I was wrongly interpreted.

When troubles arise in a friendship, we can humble ourselves before a friend and ask for forgiveness. If they choose not to accept our apology, then all we can do is continue to pray for our friend and the situation. To a degree, we are mandated to make an attempt to tie up the loose ends of a strained relationship, for Matthew 5:23–24 reads, "So if you are standing before the altar in the Temple, offering a sacrifice to God, and suddenly remember that a friend has something against you, leave your sacrifice there beside the altar and go and apologize and be reconciled to him, and then come and offer your sacrifice to God" (TLB). As Christians, we can't neglect a friendship that breaks up or cast it aside, thinking, *The whole thing is her problem.* We have a responsibility to make amends.

But just as you can't force a friendship to happen, you can't force it to be repaired either. You can offer your apologies and you can try to open the lines of communication, but there are no guarantees your efforts will mend the friendship. When apologies fall on deaf ears and there is no evidence of healing, we need to be willing to take the next step.

REALITY CHECK

You need to be honest about a friendship. Look at where it is at this moment—not where it once was or where you hope it will be. Then lay it out on the table and ask yourself, "Is it salvageable?" If you live with the illusion that everything is all right when it isn't, your sense of reality is dulled—not just in the case of the damaged friendship but in other relationships as well.

—Ruth

Learning to Let Go

For over a year and a half, I had tried in many ways to make peace between Laura and me but nothing worked. I tried my best to handle her criticism and bitterness, yet every time we were together I felt as if I were walking on eggshells. I could never please her, never make her happy. She was always irritated with me about something, and every time I left her presence I felt either guilty and depressed or tense and upset. And besides, my trying to be someone I wasn't just to please Laura was not the basis of a good friendship.

Over time I began to ask myself, "How long can I feel this way?" I had to admit the negative aspects of our friendship were draining me. Finally, I talked the situation over with my husband. He assured me that he too had noticed something different in Laura and that made me feel better. At least I knew what was happening wasn't all in my mind.

I also talked over the situation with a mutual friend. I told her what I thought was happening and she had noticed the same thing. I then asked if I was in any way fostering this bitterness in Laura. Again, I was assured that it wasn't me, but rather that Laura's critical spirit was her response to the tough personal times she was going through. My friend didn't see any more that I could do.

It was obvious I couldn't keep the friendship going. I remember saying, "Lord, I can't deal with this any longer. I give this friendship to you." And surprisingly, not long after that, Laura dropped out of my life. I didn't feel obligated to initiate contact with her—I was exhausted from the friendship. I released her without anger or hatred, and I prayed for her to be blessed. I resigned myself to the fact that our friendship could no longer be continued in its present state.

When a friendship can't be repaired by our efforts, we need to be willing to let it go. While it's hard to do, we must say, "God, I give this friendship to you. If, for some reason, it is not supposed to be part of my life, then take it out. If it *is* supposed to be a part of my life, then I pray you would restore it. Only you can bring it back and make it right." I was finally able to make a conscious, clear-headed decision based on prayer, and with the Lord's direction, I let the friendship go.

Giving It Time

God can work wonders with time, and when we are willing to let go of a relationship or situation, we give Him time to work on it. While God does His part, our part is to give a friendship the time and distance it needs and resist the temptation to force it to be healed.

GIVE A FRIEND SPACE

If a friendship starts to drift, look at what's happening in your friend's life. Often certain events drive friends apart, but these events may only be temporary circumstances. We had friends who had twins, and for nearly two years we hardly saw them because all their energy was focused on survival. In cases like this, just be patient and flexible—it doesn't always mean the friendship is over.

—Colleen

For me, the time off from my friendship with Laura, and in this case the "break" lasted nearly four years, allowed three important changes to occur. First, time gave me a chance for self-examination. I had to ask myself, "What part did I have in this?" When a friendship breaks up, each party usually contributes something to the split. With time away from Laura, the Lord opened my eyes to my role in the breakup of our friendship.

I went from having no idea what was wrong and why, to seeing ways that I had been insensitive to Laura's troubles and feelings. It took a few years to come to this realization, and when I did, I confessed it to God and asked Him to restore the relationship so I could make it up to her.

Second, time allowed the Lord to mold my heart. If I hadn't let this friendship rest, God could not have changed my heart to the degree He did. The Lord allows our hearts to break and in the process gives us a heart that is more tender. He broke down a part of my heart so I could more clearly see how abrasive my happiness in the face of Laura's sadness might have seemed to her. Because of what happened between me and Laura, I'm more aware of the times I might seem insensitive to a person and not realize it. I'm now able to apply what I've learned from this friendship to the other relationships in my life.

Finally, time allowed Laura to change as well. After our friendship broke up, the Lord worked in her life to resolve her negative feelings and critical attitude. She apologized to me for her behavior and I apologized to her for mine. Only God and time could have restored the relationship so simply and fully.

Giving It Prayer

Prayer is a major ingredient in healing a broken friendship. Not until I let go of my friendship with Laura did I really start to pray for the relationship. Prayer is powerful—it allows you to do something positive for the friendship while you patiently wait for the Lord to bring healing according to His time schedule.

When I closely examined my friendship with Laura, I still saw much of value despite the estrangement. We had a wealth of things in common and I liked and respected her as a person. As I turned this situation over to the Lord in prayer, I could see that much of what made up our friendship was honoring to Him. My friendship with Laura wasn't built on circumstances that temporarily threw us together. Our friendship was deeper than that. I was convinced my friendship with Laura was one worth praying that someday, if it were God's will, He might restore it.

Dig Deeper in the Lord

When a friendship breaks up, it helps to keep in mind the bigger perspective of how God works in our lives. He might pull a person out of your life for a time so you both can learn something.

When Laura was absent from my life, I found it hard to be without her. Despite her critical ways, she was a long-time friend. I tend to get closely connected to people, and in my closest friendships we tend to communicate openly and share each other's deepest thoughts and problems. I was thrown by the breakup in our friendship, having once been so closely connected, and I was baffled by it. I now felt like I was in the middle of an ocean by myself. It was a terrible feeling.

But with Laura gone, I had to learn to depend more on the Lord. I ended up turning to the Lord on my knees and praying, "God, there is an empty place inside me that hurts so bad. Please fill it with more of you." I'm convinced that only the Lord can fill that hole and once we allow Him to do so He brings friendships back into our lives. For me, allowing God to fill my emptiness was one opportunity for my relationship with Him to move to a greater depth. Looking back, I was able to see that good can come from a broken friendship. Where I lost in one area, I gained in another.

Renewing the Bonds

It's only been in the past few months that my friendship with Laura has been restored. I saw her one Sunday morning back at church and I knew I needed to say something. As we talked, she soon had tears in her eyes as she told me about the difficult times she and her husband had endured. It opened up the door for me to minister to her and for our friendship to be rekindled.

Both Laura and I are changed people. Her critical spirit is gone. My insensitivity is, too. She admitted she had learned a great deal in the past four years about herself and the Lord, and that she wasn't the friend she should have been. She apologized for how she had acted and asked for my forgiveness. I could see how she had softened and I know that was the Lord's work in her life. Today, I am much more aware of the level of sensitivity

I need to show her. I don't ever want to do anything to hurt her feelings again.

———— ∞ ————

As I learned from my pastor, Jack Hayford, when you give someone time and a chance to change, you need to show mercy as they attempt to restore the friendship. When Laura came back in my life I had to say, "This is a completely new person," and then give her the benefit of the doubt that God had completely changed her. Even if it had only been six months, I still needed to believe the change was genuine. We can do just that because we know it is possible for God to completely change a person in a short period of time.

It takes a mature person to say, "I let the past go. I let the negative memories go. This is a new person." With Laura, I was not going to deal with how she was. I was not going to walk on eggshells, fearful she'd soon be critical of me as she was before. Rather, I proceeded as though she were a new person. While it may be awkward to approach someone who has hurt us in the past, we can do so with prayer. As a friendship is reestablished, we have to pray every step of the way and say, "Lord, show me what steps to take and when."

When I first saw Laura at church and she was in tears and very humble, it was easy to extend a comforting hand. Restoring a friendship isn't always that easy. Even so, we shouldn't be afraid to be the first to extend ourselves. But we must do it prayerfully and with the leading of the Holy Spirit, rather than bounding into someone's life in the flesh. When the Spirit directs our actions, we can have a confidence in what we're doing and an insulation of sorts around our feelings. That way if we are rejected in our attempts at reconciliation, we know we've obeyed God and we need to keep praying. Chances are that friend is still hurting and needs more healing time.

———— ∞ ————

Not all broken friendships can be repaired or return to a level of friendship that once existed. Laura and I were fortunate. While our friendship is different because we no longer live near each other, it is now deeper than it was before. And because of my experience with Laura, I've learned just how fragile friendship can be.

If a friendship isn't to be restored, then we need to continue to hand the situation over to the Lord. I believe God puts us in contact with certain people and then moves us on as a means of teaching us what we need to know. However, if you strongly feel in your heart that a friendship should be restored, definitely tell the Lord about it and say, "God, I really do want to be a good friend to this person. I really want to be close again." Ask the Lord to restore it, and I believe He will. If nothing else, we can count on God to give us a sense of peace one way or another about the friendships He brings into our lives.

Make It Happen

1. If there is a broken friendship in your life, examine what you may have contributed to the breakup. Even if the friendship dissolved years ago and you don't have any intention of restoring it, for personal growth you need to look at your role in the relationship. Remember, it's often tough to be honest with your own faults. Pray that the Lord will soften your heart and open your eyes so that in the future you might become a better friend through what you learn about yourself.

2. Some friendships can be damaged beyond repair. If the depth of the transgression is so great—say a serious breach in trust—and the friendship cannot stand up under the weight of it, it's probably better to let it go. Forgiveness must happen in any case, but the expectation that things will return to normal should be released. Even if the friendship is reestablished, it will not be exactly the same as it was before. There will have to

be a new, deeper level of forgiveness and commitment flowing through it, and, for some people, the effort to do that may be too great. It may be easier to let it go.

3. Humility is a life-long lesson we each must learn, and it is also an ingredient in a good friendship. How is your ego when it comes to friendship? Are you living your life in accordance with Philippians 2:3, "Do nothing out of selfish ambition or vain conceit, but in humility consider others better than yourselves"? If not, make it a prayer request that through God's Word you might learn more about humility and how you can deepen this character trait within your life.

Friends on the Mend
Dee Brestin

A best friend is a gift from God, and when the bond is broken, we desperately want to mend it.

A breach between best friends is undoubtedly the most painful way for a friendship to end. What makes this so painful is that a breach occurs only when there's been a special bond between kindred spirits, like that described in 1 Samuel 18:1: "... Jonathan became one in spirit with David, and he loved him as himself."

In her book *Just Friends* (Harper & Row), Lillian Rubin describes this bond perfectly: "Best friends have the power to help and to hurt that no one but a mate can match." The pain from the demise of a best friendship is similar to the pain in divorce. There is a sense of betrayal, followed by a terrible loneliness and sense of loss.

If we truly value that friendship, then we'll want to preserve it. If you're reeling from a breach in a friendship, and want to restore it, here are some tips.

The Mending Attempt

A sincere "I love you and I'm sorry" can go a long way. As an imitator of Christ, it's always my move to initiate reconciliation, even if I perceive the fault to be on the other side.

If some sort of restitution is needed, that should be done as well. Even if we don't perceive the wound to be as deep as our friend does, love demands we be responsive to each other's pain. When Esther heard that Mordecai was in sackcloth and ashes, "she was in great distress" (Esther 4:4), and would not rest until she discovered the reason for her friend's pain. The ensuing communication between Esther and her cousin is a model of love, honesty, and responsiveness.

Eggshells

If the breach is severe, picture it as a gaping wound in your friendship. You can't hurry the healing of a scab. Expect to walk on eggshells while trust is rebuilding. This is an extremely vulnerable time.

If you're in a delicate situation, keep the following in mind:

- Don't pick at the scab or continually rehash the argument. That slows the healing process.
- Try hard to prevent infection by keeping the wound clean. After two of my friends, Debby and Jane, argued and reconciled over Jane's continual tardiness, Jane tried hard to be on time for her future lunch dates with Debby.
- Apply salve occasionally. Talk over a dessert, remember her birthday, or call to see how she's doing.
- If the wound seems to be getting worse, give your friend space. Remember, Paul and Barnabas took separate trips, but later reconciled.
- Pray for the Great Physician to apply His healing hand to your friendship wound. If possible, try praying together for the healing of your friendship.
- Increase your patience by recalling the many wonderful times you've had together. Think about all the things you value in your friend and how she's been loyal to you in the past. One day, if you do not grow weary of doing good (Galatians 6:9), the scab will fall off naturally, and the skin will be healthy again.

Closing the Door

If months, or perhaps years, have passed, and the breach hasn't mended, lay the friendship down before the Lord, for it is possible Satan is using this breach to divert your energy from a higher calling. As long as you have been tender and patient with the wound, and kept the door open for complete healing, then there is no sin on your part.

When there are two wills involved, reconciliation is not always possible, despite your best attempts. But I believe reconciliation is likely when you apply these principles, and definitely worth the sacrifice, for best friendships are priceless.

—From *Today's Christian Woman* (November/December 1990)

8

How Can I Overcome the Pain of Losing a Friend?

—Stormie Omartian

FOUR YEARS AGO, in the brief period of about twelve months, I lost three dear friends through a variety of circumstances. As I mentioned in the previous chapter, my friend Laura and I were driven apart by her unresolved bitterness and my insensitivity. In another friendship, a series of personal decisions we each made caused us to separate. And finally, my dearest and oldest friend, Diane, died of cancer. The losses were monumental. Suddenly the three women who meant the most to me were no longer part of my life.

―――――― ∾ ――――――

Of the three losses, losing Diane was, of course, the most final and painful. Our friendship was a deep bond that went back twenty-eight years to our high school days. She was like a sister to me. When she died I felt as though the bottom had dropped out of my life. I remember thinking, *Never again will anyone know me as well as Diane did.*

Not until after the funeral did the reality—and the finality—of what had happened hit me. At first, I didn't see how I could possibly recover from the loss. For more than a year I continually felt on the verge of tears, with

111

an ever-present lump in my throat. After a year, the pain started to subside and then it still took another year for that lump to completely go away.

I've found that there is nothing wrong with feeling a sense of hurt over the loss of a friend. It's a cleansing work that happens every time you feel a sense of sadness over your loss. That pain creates a certain tenderness in your heart and that's a good sign. It reminds you of what the friendship was—both the value of it and the intensity of it. It affirms that a real sense of connection took place in the relationship. And when that level of connection occurs, you cannot avoid a sense of pain over the loss of that person in your life.

Remember Who's in Charge

At the time of Diane's death, I remember reading Oswald Chambers' words in *My Utmost for His Highest* (Barbour). Chambers believed that God allows friends to move out of our life so that we can be filled with more of Him.

As I adjusted to the losses in my life, it gave me great comfort to know that I was going to be filled with more of the Lord—He wasn't just going to leave me floating in space with a gaping hole in my heart.

Just as the Lord is in charge of the formation of our friendships, He is in charge of the loss of a friend as well. I'm not saying He's to blame for the painful losses but rather, as I discovered, He will replace our losses with more of himself, and with new friendships.

Not until Diane died did I realize how dependent I was on her for emotional support. Looking back, it probably wasn't healthy to be so dependent on one friend. With the loss of two other friends at the same time, all I could do was draw closer to the Lord and rely more on Him.

I remember praying, "God, be the Lord of these relationships, and of my heart, which is hurting so badly. Somehow bring good out of this and help me to learn from it." I believe when we ask God to bring good out of something He will. Granted, it may be very painful going through the process to get to the good, but the Lord always makes something rich out of our pain.

The good I experienced from the loss of my friends was a deeper relationship with the Lord. My faith grew as I again and again felt the Lord's presence in my time of mourning. I knew that despite my pain there would be a future—that God would care for me by meeting my friendship needs. For instance, when Diane died it became obvious there were gaping holes in my relationship with my husband in terms of friendship. I remember sitting on a bed in our guest room, talking to the Lord about my pain—reading my Bible and praying—when Michael walked into the room.

I was crying and I told him I didn't know if I could live with such sadness from losing my best friend. Then he said, "I'll try to be a best friend to you." I was so touched by what he said and so appreciated his gesture. As a result, we have become much better friends than we were before.

Keep Your Heart Supple

If I'd chosen to harden my heart over the losses of my three friends, I doubt the Lord could have worked in my life as He did. Looking back, I easily could have said, "I don't want to be hurt again by losing a friend so I'm not going to allow myself to get close to anyone." If I'd hardened my heart in that way, I wouldn't have the wonderful and rich new friendships I have today. What stops our negative emotions from ruling our lives is keeping our hearts open to how God is going to work restoration in our lives. To be open to God, we need to lay our pain and needs before Him. I remember praying after the loss of Diane, "God, help me. As you have promised in your Word, please replace and fill these losses in my life."

I believe that if we're in communication with the Lord we're less likely to blame Him for the loss or the pain we feel, or worse, be tempted to shut ourselves off from God—the only One through whom real healing can come. If you are honestly entrusting every relationship to the Lord, then you'll be much less likely to develop a bitter or cynical spirit when you lose a friend.

For example, if a friendship starts to drift, as did one of my friendships, the first place we need to go is before the Lord, asking Him, "God, show me what's wrong with this relationship. Help me to see things clearly." Before the Lord, I'll become repentant if I've been in error. Or if a friend is in error, then I'll be led to pray for her. I've learned that without turning things over to the Lord, our pain can go inward and tie us in knots, but when we're open with the Lord our pain can soften our hearts.

Learn to Reach Out

If we want God to fill the holes in our lives, besides keeping our hearts soft we need to take the risk of extending ourselves in friendship and responding positively to those who extend themselves to us.

EMBRACE THE RISK

Jesus took a risk when He asked three of His followers to go with Him to the Garden of Gethsemane to stand watch with Him and pray. During that time, He took a risk of sharing His feelings and concerns only to have His friends disappoint Him. On three separate occasions the men who accompanied Him failed to stand watch or listen—instead they fell asleep. But Jesus still took the risk.

—Colleen

After losing my three close friends, I at first closed myself off to others. But the problem with a "no-risk" attitude is you also shut off opportunities for the richness a friend can bring to your life. Once I realized what I was doing I worked at remaining open to the opportunities for friendship God placed in my life. I literally had to say, "Okay, I'm willing to take the chance of being hurt because I know in the end it will be worth it. I know it's better to risk some pain than never to have known the richness of friendship."

Still, I wondered, *Who can I develop a close friendship with?* I started talking to God about my concern, and over time the Lord worked in my heart, directing me to form a prayer group of six or seven women. I remember saying, "God, I need your guidance on which women to include because I don't know who will fit well together." One by one the Lord revealed them to me, and His judgment, as usual, was perfect.

Several of these women were sympathetic to my loss of Diane and extended themselves in friendship. I'll never forget the sweet way in which one friend said, "I know I can never be Diane to you, but I believe the Lord is going to give you a number of friends, each one of which will embody one of the qualities you liked most about Diane. Please consider my hand extended as a part of that plan." Today, this woman is a treasured friend in the Lord. If I hadn't prayed for an open heart and been willing to take a risk, I'm sure I would have avoided these gestures of friendship and closed off what turned out to be major deliverance from pain and grief.

Don't Hold on Too Tight

When I was a child my family frequently moved and my life lacked consistency and security. As a result, I have a strong desire to stay in one place and I don't like it when friends move away. While my desire is for everything to stay the same, I know that's absolutely impossible. Life doesn't work that way.

To keep my heart from becoming brittle with the pain that changing friendships can bring, I've worked at not hanging on too tightly to someone. I've found that the tighter I hang onto a friendship, the more difficult it gets. I have to release my grip—to expect my friends to possibly be gone sometime in the future and to enjoy them while I still can.

RELEASING THE GRIP

Sometimes we try too hard to make a friendship happen, or to change a friend. That's when we become controlling. Friendships, like everything else in our lives, need to be handed over to God. That way He can make them what they need to be.

—Ruth

If you have to keep every relationship exactly the same, you run the risk of missing out on the change the Lord has planned for you. We need to be willing to let friendships go where they may. This won't prevent us from being hurt, but it often prevents us from being devastated by the loss of a friendship.

For instance, when someone has to leave the prayer group, I work hard at letting that friend go. Rather than focus on a friend leaving, I choose to focus on how thankful I am for the time she was in the prayer group. Not long ago, one member's husband was transferred to Atlanta. I still remember how tough it was to face the fact she was leaving. I knew there was no way I could go through the experience without it being painful, yet, while it was painful, I was able to release Patti and leave it with the Lord. I found a comfort in knowing the Lord was taking care of the situation—He was part of it—and it was this sense of comfort that allowed me to maintain a relaxed grasp.

───────── ✐ ─────────

Because God loves us we can be confident that He will care for us when we experience the pain of losing a friend. If you do lose a friend—like my friend Patti who moved to Atlanta, like Laura who went away angry, like my friend who drifted, or like Diane who died—realize that such losses, though they are painful, open up a whole new area of friendship possibilities.

The new and valued friendships I have formed in the past four years could not have happened unless others had moved out of my life. Of course, I couldn't see how this marvelous pattern of God's caring and concern would fall into place until after the fact, but today I'm convinced that God takes care of us better than we can ever imagine.

Let God take the pain in your heart and turn it into something good. Only He can do that. Four years ago, when I lost so many friends at once, I felt wiped out emotionally. I wasn't sure I'd ever be the same again. Today, my wonderful new friends are proof that God does bring good out of the pain we feel when dear friends move on.

Make It Happen

1. If you've recently lost a friend, give yourself time to heal—six months, a year if necessary. Allow yourself to feel the pain that comes with loss. Talk to others about how you feel. Above all, remember to openly share your pain with the Lord in prayer.

2. While we need to extend ourselves in friendship as well as be open to the gestures of friendship from others, don't force yourself to do too much too fast. Make sure your motives for building a new friendship are pure—a

concern for the other person, mutual interests, a leading from the Lord—not merely a desire to have someone to fill the void in your life.

3. Change is a given—especially in human relationships. Learn to focus on the one eternal constant in our world of change: the Lord. Hebrews 13:8 reads, "Jesus Christ is the same yesterday and today and forever." While we can't prevent change in our lives, we can develop an eternal perspective as a way of coping with the inevitable losses we'll experience in life.

Necessary Losses
Janis Long Harris

Many years ago, the writer of Ecclesiastes observed that "there is a time for everything and a season for every activity under heaven." In other words, God created a natural rhythm in this earth—an ebb and flow that affects everything—including friendships. Yet sometimes the changes are accompanied by a sense of loss, hurt, or guilt. But it doesn't have to be that way. Here are a few suggestions for coping with the changing seasons in friendship:

Don't deny your feelings. Even though changing friendships are a part of life, they still can cause painful feelings. And sometimes these feelings can take us by surprise. Denying or squelching these feelings won't make them go away, so allow yourself to hurt for a while. Try reading the Psalms, which eloquently express the feelings of abandonment, grief, and loneliness many of us experience in the wake of a changed or lost friendship.

Avoid placing blame on yourself or your friend. It's important to recognize that changes in friendship aren't necessarily anyone's fault. Dwelling on feelings of bitterness, resentment, or guilt is rarely productive. Someone once observed that the healthiest response to the loss or significant change of a friendship is to realize God gives us friends for a limited time. We can avoid a lot of pain if we appreciate the gift of friendship while it lasts and be willing to accept a new gift in a new time.

Seek new friends in each season. New places in life can often bring new friends. Just ask the new mom who's feeling the loss of her office friendships. "I finally decided to *do* something instead of just feel bad," one woman said. "I've taken steps to replace some of the friendships I've lost with people who are in circumstances similar to mine."

Anticipate the changes that may come with a new season of life and prepare for them. Lauren was completely unprepared for the friendship void she experienced after quitting work to stay home with her new baby. She got so desperate that one spring day she sat on the front porch and called out to the first woman she saw pushing a stroller—a complete stranger—and invited her in for a cup of coffee.

One woman, now in her late fifties, has experienced the changes in friendship that come with marriage, children, an empty nest and, most recently, retirement. Her advice on how to prepare is, "First, choose some friends who aren't in the same place you are, people you can share, laugh, and have fun with, but who are in very different life circumstances. I think it's important to get a different viewpoint about life. And second, it's helpful to cultivate friends who have already experienced what you're about to, who can offer insights into some of the things you'll be going through."

Recognize that each season has its own rewards. While one woman misses the intensity of the friendships she had with other women before she became a mother, she's learned to appreciate the gifts her current season of life brings.

"I've decided it's more important to spend large amounts of time with my children at this point in my life," she explains. "When they get to be teenagers, spending a lot of time with Mom isn't going to be a high priority for them. So it's a trade-off."

—From *Today's Christian Woman* (July/August 1991)

9

Why Do I Always Tend to Compare Myself With My Friends?

—Ruth Senter

THERE WAS A TIME when I felt fairly insecure about my interior decorating skills. In the past twenty-seven years I've probably bought every kind of country living magazine printed because not only do I enjoy the pictures, but I needed the practical helps as well. As a result of my insecurity about home decorating, I often found myself making comparisons between my friends' homes and my own.

Our tendency to compare is nothing new—it all started in Genesis 3 when Eve was tempted by the serpent with something she wanted but didn't have—fruit from the tree of knowledge of good and evil. It's human nature to want what we don't have—in my case a natural flair for interior decorating. However, as Christians we need to remind ourselves of the teaching of gifts in 1 Corinthians 12:12–31. In this passage, Paul likens the gifts to parts of the body, with all the gifts working together for the good of the whole.

Unfortunately, in our humanness we sometimes feel that another's gift—the ability to decorate a home or to create a meal that's a work of art—will somehow diminish our own gift rather than contribute to it or bring it out. Within friendships, constant comparisons of our gifts have several serious consequences.

Danger Ahead

First, comparisons can make us blind to our own gifts and how our gifts can work together with a friend's. If another's gift only reminds us of what we don't have, we can't enjoy that person's gift.

In college I had a friend who was genuinely funny. Everything that came out of her mouth made me laugh. We worked together at a little ceramic tile shop on Wells Street in Chicago. In response to her funny stories, I think I felt the need to entertain her with equally funny stories. One day it dawned on me—I couldn't enjoy her stories because I was working so hard on my stories, which didn't come nearly as easily. I learned a significant lesson that year—I needed her to lighten my life and it was okay to relax and enjoy her gift. I didn't need to compete.

My inability to relax and enjoy in that case leads me to another closely-related danger of comparisons—one-upmanship. I recall the time someone asked me about a mission trip our family had taken to Venezuela. Before I could say more than two sentences she launched into the story of her family's mission trip to Mexico. The message was clear—she didn't really want to hear about our trip to Venezuela. Instead, she seemed to want to compare her experiences with ours. Unfortunately, I'm sure I've done the same with others, sometimes without even being aware of it.

———— ✐ ————

Second, comparisons make us terribly dissatisfied with ourselves. For instance, back when I was struggling with feelings of insecurity over my home decorating abilities, when I visited a friend's home, rather than notice the beauty, I might instead focus on the stenciled border she did—all the time thinking of my borderless walls at home. Such comparisons caused me to forget what I had accomplished in my home. For the moment I'd forget that I, too, had gifts—just gifts in different areas.

Comparisons caused me to place the focus back on myself. It's hard for me to appreciate another person when she reminds me of what I'm not. And when I run everything about the other person through a filter of "me and how am I doing," such comparisons insidiously begin to erode my self-esteem. Such thinking is destructive to my own sense of self-worth and personal confidence.

Third, comparisons cause me to become critical of the other person even though I may be in awe of her at the same time. If you always think of yourself in comparison to another, in the long run you'll have to put the other person down to move yourself up. As you observe a friend's gifts, you may genuinely compliment your friend, but on closer look, your compliment may also contain a personal put-down.

THE COMPARISON TRAP

Comparisons caused a serious breach in one friendship of mine. My friend's constant comparisons lead to the point of jealousy on her part and, after a while, just being in her presence was draining for me. I felt so uncomfortable always knowing that accomplishments were bringing out a sense of jealousy in her that finally I had to let the friendship rest.

—Stormie

Some years ago, I had a friend who could create meals like those pictured in magazines. When she invited company over, her table was beautiful and loaded with homemade goodies. One evening we were invited to dinner and as I saw the spread before me, I made a comment like, "We hit the Golden Arches last night at our house."

My friend stopped, looked at me, and said, "Ruth, I'm serving you this dinner tonight not to outdo you but to tell you how much I love you." Her words stopped me. I let her comment sink in. Until that moment I hadn't realized my tendency to compare myself to her.

A few weeks later when we met for coffee, I brought up her comment for discussion. "What clues did you have that I was comparing myself with you?" I asked. She said that my compliments regarding her gifts sometimes contained comparisons. Even though I thought I was only putting down myself with my flip comment about the "Golden Arches," in reality I was putting down my friend and causing her to feel uncomfortable about her gift. I then realized that I needed to view her dinners and homemade goodies as a gift to me—a genuine expression of love—not as a means of outdoing me or making me feel inferior.

———— ✑ ————

Finally, comparisons can become a barrier to friendship because they cause us to categorize others and ourselves. When we operate on preconceived notions of what someone else is or what we are not, which may not be based in fact, we prevent ourselves from discovering what we might have in common with someone despite our outward differences.

A number of years ago I attended a dinner where a former beauty queen sat three seats down from me. She was a gorgeous woman as well as an outstanding Christian. I remember looking at her lovely nails and trying to keep my own unpolished nails hidden under the table as much as possible throughout the meal. Beyond that, I knew the outfit I was wearing wasn't in my most flattering colors. For the duration of the evening all I could think was, *My nails aren't polished and I'm wearing the wrong colors.*

At the end of the meal this woman came up to me and said, "Ruth, I've wanted to meet you for some time and tell you how much your writing has touched my heart." She went on to tell me how something I had written had restored her confidence in God during a very difficult time in her life. I was absolutely speechless. I had no idea this woman even knew my name.

That night I realized comparisons, if we let them, can keep us from reaching out to others.

Avoiding the Comparison Trap

While comparing ourselves to others comes naturally, it is a habit we can break. To begin with we need to start with right thinking because from right thinking comes right actions. Consider for a moment what you think of yourself. Are most of your thoughts about yourself negative? Mine certainly were the night I shared a table with the former beauty queen. All I could think about was my own appearance. I could have been thinking, "I'm here for a reason. This evening is a gift from God and there might be a life I can touch tonight."

We must learn to think the way God thinks about us. Paul reminds us of the value of positive thinking about ourselves in Ephesians 2:10 when he says, "For we are God's workmanship, created in Christ Jesus to do good works, which God prepared in advance for us to do." The word "workmanship" in Greek is *poema*, the root of our English word for "poem." A poem is a literary work of art, and I believe Paul chose that word deliberately to say to us, "You need to look at yourself as God's work of art because you're created for good works." Understanding this fact is the basis of a healthy and positive self-esteem. If we feel positive about who we are in Christ, we won't need to compare ourselves with others.

We'll be less likely to compare ourselves with our friends if we're content. Paul writes in 1 Timothy 6:6, "Godliness with contentment is great gain." One of the gains of contentment comes in my relationships with others. If I'm content with myself, then I can appreciate another's gifts without feeling mine are somehow inferior. I must be open to how a friend's gifts can enrich my life and I need to realize that I don't have to duplicate a friend's gift. Only when I learned to accept my college friend's gift of humor rather than try to outdo her could my life be enriched by her.

Beyond contentment and right thinking, we need to monitor our words. Not until my friend pointed out that my compliments about her cooking ability were actually comparisons that put us both down did I even realize what I was doing. She helped me see that while I might notice the comparison, I'm better off not adding it to my compliment. Indirectly I may have been trying to laugh at myself or show my friend I didn't think more highly of myself than I ought to. It's one thing to tell a joke on yourself, but when a friend's gift is part of the joke, the compliment actually devalues you and your friend at the same time.

One tool that has helped me change my thinking and my choice of words is journaling. As I reflect on my day, I often catch blind spots. I might realize I said something that contained a comparison statement or that I'd been putting myself down in my attitude. And if I jot down my reflections, I'm more likely to remember next time comparisons rear their ugly head.

FOCUSING ON THE GIFTS

We should help a friend focus on her strengths, not her weaknesses. We should overlook a friend's deficits and hope she does the same for us. Solid, lasting friendships build on the good.

—Colleen

The Blessing of Comparisons

Not all comparisons are bad. In some cases, the comparisons we draw can be helpful. I have looked at my mother through the years and have benefitted from her quiet, gentle spirit. Every time I'm with her I admire her peacefulness and I desire to be like her. My comparisons with my mother have helped me to be more gentle and have moved me beyond my more natural brash and impetuous personality. God has used my mother to soften me.

I once had the privilege of interviewing a woman whose husband had been murdered, leaving her with three small children to raise. As I talked with the woman, I could see contentment in her face. And I came away from our time together not dissatisfied with myself but challenged because I saw qualities in her that I wanted to develop in myself—godly qualities such as a sense of gratefulness, joy, and contentment.

Within our friendships comparisons will be made, but we have a choice as to whether they'll be a blessing or a curse. If the comparisons only leave us feeling disappointed with ourselves—always reminding us of what we don't have or can't do—then we need to work at eliminating such comparisons. However, if the comparisons motivate us toward building a more Christlike character then we need to look at them as God working more of His grace into our lives.

Make It Happen

1. In what areas do you tend to feel inadequate and insecure? Is it home decorating, wearing the right clothes, styling your hair, or gardening? Once you are aware of your weak spots, realize that in situations where a friend shines with a talent you are lacking, your natural response will be to feel envy. Learn to recognize envy and squelch it before it has a chance to grow.

2. Quickly jot down your top three strengths—those abilities and talents with which you feel God has specifically blessed you. If you're stumped, think of what you most like to do and are best at doing. The next time you feel yourself falling into a comparison trap, remind yourself of your list. While you might not have all the special abilities of a friend, God has given you different and specific talents for a reason. Rather than focus on comparing yourself with others, focus on how you can put these strengths in action to advance God's work on earth.

3. Think for a moment what the world would be like if we all shared the same gifts and talents. Life would become monotonous. Be grateful to God for the variety of abilities and talents He has woven into His children and the opportunities we each have to enjoy this variety through many friends.

4. If you notice a talent in a friend that lacks polish in your own life, consider asking that friend for some help in developing the potential you have in that area. For your friend it will be a blessing to share something she enjoys, for you a challenge to learn something new. Together it's a great opportunity to strengthen the bonds of friendship.

Circle of Approval
Janis Long Harris

Peer pressure: it can make us act on other women's values instead of our own. Or forget our priorities. That's particularly troublesome when we've tried to conform our values to Christian principles. Learning to resist peer pressure can have some tremendous benefits, both to ourselves and others. One benefit is an exhilarating sense of freedom, as one woman discovered when she made a conscious decision to stop worrying about what other people think.

It's one thing to conclude that it's important to live your life without undue concern for what other people think. It's another thing to do it. Here are some principles I've found helpful.

Make the decision to resist negative peer pressure. "I'm making a conscious effort to care less about what other people think and how they're rating me," says Anne, who has struggled with peer pressure in the past. "For example, when I'm disciplining my children, I try to base what I'm doing on what's good for my child rather than on what other people think is the way it should be handled. In a given situation, I ask myself, 'Am I getting angry at my child because she's not meeting someone else's expectations or because she really needs to be disciplined?'"

Narrow your circle of approval. While few people are impervious to the opinions of others, some women have been able to narrow the circle of those whose approval they seek, like women in their prayer group or Sunday school class.

Distinguish between negative, positive, and neutral peer pressure. Peer pressure isn't always bad. Consider the situation of my friend Kim, who is so resistant to peer pressure that she doesn't even dress up for more formal events.

"I tend to set pretty easygoing standards for myself, so peer pressure makes me shape up—to get my degree, do more volunteer work, join a health club and exercise," admits Kim. "For me, peer pressure is almost always good."

When peer pressure is neither good nor bad, some women choose to conform rather than expend the effort to resist conformity. Diane, for example, is uncomfortable with the way her friends hug each other at church and social gatherings. She could tell them she's just not that demonstrative and would rather maintain a friendly distance. But because she knows they're expressing genuine warmth and affection, she goes along with the custom.

Learn the difference between Christian concern for the feelings of others and an unhealthy obsession with what others are thinking of you. "Some people think they're showing care for others' feelings when what they're really concerned about is conforming to others' expectations," points out pastoral counselor Bonnie Niswander. "To care about what others think and grow from it is different than worrying about what others think of you."

Draw on your spiritual resources. "Prayer is one way I resist peer pressure," says Pam. "When I take my concerns to God, just the act of doing that releases me from a lot of concern about what other people think."

Remember whose approval really counts. "So much of our mindset is geared to seeking the approval of others," observes Julie. "Seeking God's approval doesn't come as naturally. But I'm finally coming to realize that happiness has to be related to doing what's right for God."

As a Christian, my goal is to become more sensitive to the right kind of pressure—the gentle promptings of the Lord who created me and offers me the strength I need to live a life that pleases Him.

—From *Today's Christian Woman* (January/February 1991)

10

How Can I Make Long-Distance Friendships Work?

—Colleen Evans

EACH SPRING IN CALIFORNIA, thousands of little buds will blossom on each mature orange tree, and for each bud there exists the potential for an orange to grow. Obviously, one tree can't support that many oranges and soon dozens of the buds drop. As the buds fall to the ground we're inclined to think, *There go all the oranges.* What we don't realize is that now more concentrated energy can go toward the development of the oranges that remain.

And so it is to a degree with long-distance friendships. In the course of our lives with Louie as a pastor, we've moved several times, twice across the country, and with those moves we've had to leave many valued friends behind. Over time some of those friendships have dropped away like orange blossoms simply because the tree of our life couldn't support that many long-distance friendships. However, a few of those friendships have remained and matured over the years. The reason some blossoms must drop is because long-distance friendships require a great deal of time, effort, and energy on our part—something each of us has in limited supply.

Because it's natural and healthy for a fruit tree to lose

blossoms, we can't feel bad when some blossoms fall. In the Bible Jesus spoke of entire branches being pruned back. John 15:1–2: "I am the true vine, and my Father is the gardener. He cuts off every branch in me that bears no fruit, while every branch that does bear fruit he prunes so that it will be even more fruitful." If we prune the branches of our many relationships then the remaining fruit will be more flavorful, zesty, and sweet.

In many cases, distance has made me realize how precious certain friendships are and that I want to continue to invest in these friendships—despite the miles between us. But we need to realize we can only hold so many people close to our hearts. With the extra effort required for a long-distance friendship we should expect to have only a few that are truly quality friendships.

Won't We Drift Apart?

One concern we often have with a long-distance friendship is the loss of intimacy. After all, we no longer see our friend on a daily or weekly basis and know the ins and outs of her life. But friendship doesn't require that we see the person every week. We get trapped into thinking intimacy equals frequency of being together.

Years ago, before I was married, I had a tightly knit group of women friends. However, after I was married my priorities changed and I wasn't as free to go to lunch or do some of the other fun things we once did as a group. For some of the women, who equated intimacy with meeting regularly, our friendship lapsed. But for others it continued, because they understood the expectations they once held for our friendship had changed and they didn't try to make demands on me that I couldn't meet.

Besides adjusted expectations for intimacy in our friendships, another factor that contributes to continued intimacy is the type of friendship you're hoping to nurture. If your long-distance friendship is with a soulmate and you worked long and hard on the friendship before the miles separated you, chances are good the level of intimacy will remain. With soul-mates, when we touch one another again—through letters, calls, or a visit—the relationship will always be there, it won't be something we need to rebuild with each contact.

Our covenant group of couples from our years in Washington, D.C., is one set of friends we cry with, laugh with, play with, and pray with. We have gone through so much together and we never want to lose our sense of closeness. Within our covenant group is one couple we're especially close to. We're bonded in many special ways with this couple as soul-mates. Through the years and across the miles the intimacy hasn't lapsed and, as a result, we make the intentional effort to get together several times a year. With them in Oregon and us in California, we try to meet at some predetermined halfway point for a few days. Granted, this is really an investment of time, energy, and resources, but it's something each of us as a couple needs.

Meeting the Communication Challenge

Long-distance friendships are wonderful but, as I said, they take some doing. Intentionality is key to such friendships. Even more so than in other friendships, we have to be committed to keeping the friendship going. And the biggest challenge to keeping it going is finding new ways to communicate.

While there are endless ways to communicate and continue a friendship, two that work best for me are pictures and letters. Most of the pictures on my refrigerator are of long-distance friends. This way, whenever I'm in the kitchen I'll see their faces and think of them. Besides, if I can see a friend's face, even if it's only a photo, somehow the distance between us doesn't feel so great.

I prefer letter-writing because I'm comfortable with that medium. However, I do have friends who aren't letter-writers and instead prefer to call. Marge, a friend I've known for more than thirty years, is like this. Marge and I met when Louie and I were in Scotland at the University of Edinburgh. Now with Marge living in New York, I hear from her maybe twice a year and always try to see her if I'm in the area. Marge is great on the phone and that's how we keep tabs on each other—she once even suggested we set up a standard time to call.

However you choose to communicate, take the time to log in with one another. And by logging in I mean let your long-distance friend know where you are on the core issues—your thoughts and feelings—not just the externals like how the kids are doing or what you have planned for the day. I've found it helpful to make a list of the things I want to make sure we talk about when I do communicate with a long-distance friend—I don't want to waste time. I've noticed, too, when a distance is involved often we become more intentional about what we want to communicate—we take the time to think through the news we want to exchange.

Praying for our long-distance friends is another great way to stay in contact. The connection through the Holy Spirit is very real, and when we get a nudge to contact a friend we need to act on those nudges. I firmly believe God is able to let us know when a friend has needs, and I think that meaningful things happen in the lives of our friends that wouldn't otherwise happen if we didn't pray for them.

When I see the pictures I have of my friends on my refrigerator, quite often I'll say a quick prayer for each, asking God's blessing on that person. This three-way communication between you, God, and your friend is important to a long-distance friendship. God wants to direct us even in the small ways, and He will if we desire to be led and are open to the "poke in the ribs" He sometimes gives us on a friend's behalf.

DIMINISHING THE DISTANCE

Praying for a friend is the most important thing you can do to keep a long-distance friendship close. In fact, you can be closer through prayer with a long-distance friend than with someone who lives nearby. When regularly praying in-depth for a friend, you'll find that the next opportunity you have to see or talk with your friend will seem as though no time or space has come between you.

—Stormie

While we have to be intentional about keeping the communication going, beyond that we have to be willing to say, "God, you know my needs and will see that my friendship needs are met in one way or another." I've noticed that God meets our needs for friendship in ways we sometimes can't even imagine. I'll often write to a long-distance friend saying, "I hope sometime this year God will cause our paths to cross," and surprisingly, He does. For instance, while there are only a very few friends we can take the time to plan a special trip to visit, there are many long-distance friends I see throughout the year in unexpected ways—a layover at the airport, or a business trip in the area where they live.

———— ❧ ————

Long-distance relationships won't work unless both people make the effort. If we're trying to cultivate a long-distance friendship and the friend doesn't reciprocate, we shouldn't stop communicating on our part but instead adjust some of our expectations for the friendship. In some cases, a friend may not initially respond to your attempts at continuing the friendship, but if you're consistent there will be rewards—that friend

135

may come around. It might be that she's not a good letter-writer but loves to talk on the phone like my friend Marge. Don't get discouraged, but instead work at finding the communication style that best suits your relationship.

What we get out of a long-distance friendship is equal to what we're willing to invest in it. The covenant group that I've mentioned before has made a conscious decision to invest in continuing our friendships, and, to do that, we get together twice a year. Two of the five couples, including ourselves, have moved west, so we go east once a year and spend about three days with our covenant group. Then later in the year the couples who live in the east visit us. Our getting together involves an investment of both time and money. Louie and I have to put aside money to make that trip, and it's an expense we are able to budget in for only a few long-distance friendships. But we're willing to stretch ourselves and use our time and money that way because we know how much it means to us to continue these friendships. We would be poorer as human beings if we weren't filled by these deep relationships.

Beating the Odds

Keeping a positive attitude about a friendship, despite the distance, has a lot to do with our determination to make the friendship work. We can get easily discouraged and say a long-distance friendship requires too much effort. But if it's a valuable relationship and you're willing to spend the time and energy on it, then it can work. We have a choice—we can do the activities required to keep the friendship going by remembering that friend and what's important to her world or we can let the friendship drop. But I believe if we say "yes" to the extra work a long-distance friendship requires, we will be rewarded with the richness of relationships God has planned for our lives.

SURPRISE PACKAGE

Yesterday was February 23. Cold. Gray. Depressing. That is, until I opened an envelope from a friend who lives 800 miles away. The note inside read: "I remember how long February is for you. Maybe this will help to hurry spring." The note was attached to a package of spring flower bath salts.

—Ruth

Tomorrow, Olive, a dear friend from our days in Scotland and a woman who lived with us for two years in the United States, is coming to visit. She now lives in New Zealand and I haven't seen her in eighteen years, but through letters we've stayed in touch. If it weren't for our mutual intentional effort to keep the friendship going she wouldn't be traveling all the way from Scotland, where she's visiting family, to California before she heads back to New Zealand. Olive has said in her letters, "I never realized how much it meant to me to be with your family, and how much it means to me to be able to see you all again."

As the years pass we begin to treasure relationships more. We see the value in them and we're willing to go that extra mile to see a long-distance friendship thrive. When a one-in-a-million friend comes into our lives, we don't want to let her go, no matter what the distance. Something special has happened between us, and our friend is so unique that it's worth cultivating the friendship until that blossom becomes a beautiful fruit. We are rich relationally when we have friends who mean so much we say, "Now that I've found you, no matter how many miles separate us, I'm never going to let you go!"

Make It Happen

1. Be realistic about how many long-distance friendships you can nurture—it might be no more than one or two. As you make your decision about which friendships should be given your time and energy, ask for the Lord's leading in your decision-making. Take your time in making the decision and be sensitive to those nudges from the Lord—it may take months for you to discover what long-distance friendships God has planned for your life.

2. Look for fun and unique ways to remember long-distance friends. Does your friend have a special interest or collect something unique? When you see an item that reminds you of your friend consider sending her a surprise in the mail—just to let her know you're thinking of her.

3. Find a communication style you're comfortable with and that works realistically with your schedule and other responsibilities. If writing long letters seems like an overwhelming task, then consider using small note cards or, better yet, a postcard that allows you to send out mini-updates when you get five minutes to write.

11
Are Cliques Necessarily Bad?

—Ruth Senter

WHENEVER I HEAR THE WORD "clique" I'm suddenly a third-grader again, back in Hesston, Kansas, standing on the steps of a little four-room schoolhouse. My family had recently moved from the cotton fields of Alabama to Kansas for my dad to complete his schooling. I remember coming out the door of the school that first week and seeing a circle of girls from my classroom gathered around the merry-go-round—painfully aware I was the outsider. I spoke with an accent. I was self-conscious of my clothes, light-weight and summery, which was appropriate for Alabama but not Kansas.

Not one girl invited me over to join the group and so I stood there alone on the steps. To this day, I vividly remember how devastated I felt to be excluded.

At some time or another, we've all had negative feelings about cliques because we've been hurt by one. For most, cliques evoke a more negative than positive image because they usually involve someone being excluded. However, that said, a clique, in its simplest form, is basically an interest group. Everybody is part of a clique in some way, shape, or form—it might be your family, a group from church, or a group of mothers with preschoolers.

For instance, I love England and naturally gravitate toward people who are interested in that country. I could easily spend hours talking with someone who shares my same interest. And likewise, with my son being a senior in high school, I find it much easier to talk with a mother who has a son the same age and is going through what I'm going through. We can't ignore the fact that we like to spend time with people who share our interests, our experiences, or our circumstances.

A clique, as good and as nourishing as it can be, also has the potential for deterioration and destruction for us as individuals and for others. Just the fact that cliques are so comfortable should be a warning to us that they also have their downside. Cliques in themselves aren't "bad" unless one of two things happens: they become a preoccupation, or they become public and exclude others.

One Tight Circle

A clique is affirming. It's neat to be the inside person. It's exciting. *It's safe.* And that's one of the problems. Danish philosopher and theologian Soren Kierkegaard tells a story about a flock of Canada geese on their way to Florida. The geese needed a rest and found a farmer's barnyard. The corn was so good and the barnyard so safe and protected from the wind that the next morning as they prepared to continue their trip they thought maybe an extra day in the safety of the barnyard would be good.

You can imagine what happened. The longer they stayed, the more they liked it. After a while they were so comfortable and well-fed that even if they had wanted to go to Florida they were far too full to fly. In the coming weeks, as other flocks flew over the barnyard, the sound of their honking would stir something in the geese in the barnyard. The sidetracked geese would then fly to the tree tops only to have the lure of the barnyard bring them back. In time the barnyard was so comfortable and secure, they no longer heard the honking geese above, flying south. Sad to say, they never got to Florida.

In a sense, cliques do the same for us—they provide a haven. They dull us to the sounds around us and feed into our natural instinct to stay where it's safe—with familiar faces and those with whom we have something in common. Yet we can't stay in that "barnyard" because I believe at times God would have us branch out in our relationships and "fly south."

Besides preventing us from venturing beyond the familiar, cliques can also cause us to have blind spots. Because the chemistry within a group may be so right and there are so many shared likes and interests, we can easily become drawn into the group and lose perspective. We no longer see the broader picture—that is, others outside the group who might be potential friends.

That day on the playground, as I stood on the steps, the group of little girls at the merry-go-round didn't even see me. To a certain degree the behavior of those girls was typical of third-graders and it's something most children have to survive no matter how painful. But I still see the same behavior—exclusivity—among adults today. A group of women gather at one table for a Bible study while another sits alone. The new couple at church standing near the coffeepot while a few feet away several couples exchange greetings. Members of a clique can be so involved in each other that they don't see those who stand on the fringes.

To prevent a clique from becoming a preoccupation, periodically ask yourself, "Do I know anything about others outside of my immediate group?" "Have I made any attempts to reach out to those not in my clique?" "When someone new enters our group have I made an attempt to talk to her, to fill her in on the context of our conversations?" If the answer is "no" to any of these questions, then more than likely you're too caught up in your group.

A good principle to follow is that anything about a relationship that comes easy has the *potential* to become bad—a flower can become a weed. Cliques are not necessarily bad in themselves, but, like the geese, we need to remember that anything that's secure and comfortable has the potential to sidetrack us from our goal. As Christians, our goal is to show care and concern for everyone—not just those with whom we share interests.

THE GOOD AND THE BAD

Cliques are bad when they limit our relationships and exclude others. However, they are not bad when they provide the love and security we need to risk reaching out to others—a risk that might lead to a heartless rejection. The unconditional love I feel from our family and our covenant group—both of which could be considered cliques—actually enables me to live inclusively in the world!

—Colleen

Members Only

Cliques can become devastating to those on the outside if a group gathers in a public setting—the church, the school, or the office. It's easy to see how it can happen, though. The night before you might be talking to a friend on the phone, see her the next day at church along with a few other friends in the same group, and soon you take up last night's conversation where you left off.

Cliques shouldn't have any part of a group that takes place within a bigger group context. A good rule of thumb: cliques are okay when they're conducted privately. Of course, I'm not suggesting you ignore those members in your group when you see them, say at church, but rather I'm suggesting that within a public setting you need to focus on being friendly to more than "your group."

A few years ago, when my husband was on a pastoral staff, a woman named Nelda joined our church, and after spending some time together, I realized I wanted to get to know her better. We were fast becoming good friends. She invited me to her home a few times or we met at a restaurant several towns away.

One day she called me and said, "I don't want you to think I'm ignoring you at church when I don't spend coffee hour or the Sunday school hour with you. I understand that as a pastor's wife you need to talk to many people. And since I'm a newcomer at church I need to get to know a lot of people."

I hung up the phone and thought, *Here is a wise woman.*

My friend understood cliques. Her husband's company moved him every two years and she knew from experience what it was like to be on the outside. Having moved often as a child and been on the outside, I, too, am very sensitive to the damage cliques can do.

Nelda moved away a few years later and one weekend came back to visit. At church that Sunday, Carol, a mutual friend, came up to us. "Nelda. What are you doing here?" she asked. "I'm visiting Ruth," replied Nelda. Carol looked at us in amazement and said, "I didn't know you two were good friends." Nelda and I looked at each other and smiled. Thankfully, we had avoided being looked upon as a clique.

If you're part of a clique, it's best to conduct the business of your clique in private. For instance, if the clique is a work-related one, rather than congregate around the same person's office each morning making small talk, choose to go out to lunch on occasion. Try not to leave all your group business for times you're in a public setting—talk over the phone or meet at each other's homes. The goal is to not visibly leave anyone out.

Remember, it's easy to create an insider/outsider image—even when it's not our intention. One devastating statement I heard from behind a pulpit came when a minister talked consistently about his best friend. In my mind I wondered which members of the congregation were his best friends—the insiders—and which were his surface friends—the outsiders. If you have a public platform of any kind, it is not the place to talk about your best friends because somebody will always feel left out. If you're the president of the school P.T.A. and you are chairing a meeting, it is inappropriate to tell everyone present about all the wonderful ideas and discussions that have taken place within a smaller grouping of friends or colleagues.

PROCEED WITH PRAYER

God's ways are inclusive rather than exclusive and as His followers we should have His heart toward those around us. Still, it's nearly impossible to not exclude someone from something at some time. All we can do is proceed prayerfully, lovingly, and graciously in all our dealings with people and ask God to make us aware when someone might feel left out.

—Stormie

We will belong to cliques, we will have best friends—Jesus did—but we need to be careful how we talk about these relationships in the presence of another who may be wistfully standing on the outside looking in. Keep your eyes peeled for the lonely people. Not that you have to be friends with everyone, but within a public setting look for opportunities to learn all kinds of new and interesting things about the new and interesting people who cross your path.

Moving From the Outside to the Inside

Our natural instinct is to want to be included in a group. If you find yourself desiring to be part of the "in group" in the neighborhood, at church, or school, the first question you need to ask yourself is, *Why do I want to be in?*

Does the reason stem from some sort of deprivation in your life? Maybe you aren't feeling secure in your marriage, with your family, or with a sibling. As a result you're frantically looking for a group to belong to as a way of dealing with your unresolved problems within other relationships. Before you seek membership in a group make certain that your primary relationships— your marriage and your children or your extended family—are in order. There is a tendency to try to create a family within our friendships to make up for the brokenness that might exist in our own families.

Next, check on your level of desire to belong to a certain group. Is it an obsession? Do you find yourself saying, "I just *have* to be accepted by this group." Finally, what is your motivation to be part of a group? Some women have been so hurt by cliques in the past that they don't come to a group with the intention of being a true friend, but rather as someone intent on breaking up a comfortable circle of friends.

While these are reasons to hold back from joining a certain group, there are several valid reasons to seek membership in a group. Chemistry is one reason to follow through on your desire to join. You have a natural feeling of wanting to belong and you find yourself saying, "I like this group. We're interested in the same things." Another reason is you might see possible benefits from being part of the group—shared knowledge on a common interest and the chance to learn more about that interest. Beyond that, you see where you can contribute to the good of the group.

If these are your motives for seeking membership within a group then it's fine to go about intentionally gaining access. The place to start is with one individual in the group, preferably the one person you feel the most comfortable with or have the most in common with. Get to know that person one-on-one. Invite her into your home. Talk to her on the phone. Rather than focus on the group, focus on a person in the group. As your friendship grows, the next logical step is to move to the level of getting to know that person's friends—members of the clique.

In one friendship I became close to the woman's mother. When my friend moved away, the friendship I had with her mother deepened and we then became good friends. In a sense, she and her mother were a mini-clique. Once I got to know my friend and met her mother, I realized there were many traits in her mother that I enjoyed and respected. My friendship with her mother was the next logical development of a friendship.

Once you gain a person's trust and the one-to-one friendship deepens, then you can begin to learn more about the group in general. As an outsider you can share your observations about the group with your friend, and she can gain from you a perspective on the group as well. Once you become a member of the group you'll understand the clique better, what holds them together, and why they are close friends.

———— ✑ ————

The need to be part of something bigger than yourself is human. Cliques have their upside and their downside. We must allow for our humanness and not feel guilty about our natural tendency to gravitate toward those with whom we share interests and experiences. Rather than condemn cliques, we need to have tolerance and understanding for how we operate as humans. We need to give ourselves permission to have special friends and belong to special groups of people. But at the same time we need to be aware of the potential pain cliques can cause and look for ways we can keep cliques a positive part of friendship.

Make It Happen

1. Do any of your friendships exhibit the signs of being a clique—shared interests, experiences, or circumstances? If you were an outsider, how would you view your clique? Is it positive—one that is open to others and accepting of newcomers or is it one that gives people the distinct impression that they are the "outsider"? If so, take steps to broaden your perspective by choosing not to gather exclusively with members of the clique in a public setting where others might look on longingly.

2. If you were hurt by a clique as a child or teenager, be aware that negative feelings about cliques can still be with you and taint your view of others who belong to cliques as adults. Consider writing a letter to God that describes how you felt being excluded. End with a request of the Lord to help you resolve feelings, move beyond them, and not allow them to hinder you as you develop adult friendships.

3. When you feel as though you're on the outside, regain some perspective by reminding yourself of what group you are a part of—your human family and the family of God through faith in Jesus Christ. What group membership could possibly be more important?

PART THREE

Friendship Builders

FRIENDSHIP IS NEVER an easy, automatic endeavor. As Colleen, Stormie, and Ruth have testified in the past chapters, it's ups and downs; it's successes and failures; it's a case of mastering the basics and overcoming the obstacles. And once we have the basics down we can focus on the opportunities for friendship at newer and deeper levels—those that are often the most challenging.

In the following section, Ruth and Colleen openly explore these tough areas. First, Ruth tackles speaking the truth in love to a friend—even when that truth might hurt. With wise biblical advice Ruth shows us how we can differentiate between speaking the truth based on conviction from God and doing so out of our own personal pet peeves.

Second, Colleen shares how cross-generational friendships—something that's growing rarer with today's hectic lifestyles—have enhanced her life. While not every one of us will develop a friendship with a woman our senior or junior, when we do we'll open up our hearts and our lives to a richness that, as Colleen says, "I never would have expected."

And finally, Colleen shares her insights and experiences on one of the toughest friendship matches—couple friendships. With couple friendships it's not just a two-way match, but instead a four-way match—seldom an easy task.

May this final section give you the encouragement and knowledge necessary to take your friendships to new and exciting levels.

12

How Can I Speak the Truth in Love and Still Maintain a Friendship?

—Ruth Senter

IN THE PAST, a dear friend has sometimes had to say some seemingly hard things to me, and likewise I've had to say a few such words to her, yet we still have a healthy friendship—one we've maintained for many years. The honest words we sometimes exchange are not said because we want to be picky, critical, or point out some petty preference we have, but rather said out of true love and conviction. When we've had to say hard things, we always know it is for the good of the other person.

———— ∾ ————

We need to give ourselves permission to say the hard things that will hold a friend accountable—after all, it's biblical. Proverbs has a lot to say about accountability between friends. Proverbs 15:22 puts it in the context of counseling, "Plans fail for lack of counsel, but with many advisers they succeed." Our holding someone accountable is part of helping her succeed by seeing things she might not otherwise see.

Proverbs 27:17 reads, "As iron sharpens iron, so one

man sharpens another." When I read this verse I have the image of the blacksmith I once saw in colonial Williamsburg, Virginia. For the iron to become sharp the sparks had to fly.

Proverbs 27:6 reads, "Wounds from a friend can be trusted." Jesus understood the concept of letting His friends go through pain at times, such as not rushing to Mary and Martha's side when their brother Lazarus was dying (John 11). While our actions or words might seem harsh to a friend, it may be something that friend needs. Often a friend's emotions have led her astray or she's blinded to the obvious because she's too close to the situation.

For the honesty necessary for accountability to take place, a sense of trust and respect is necessary among friends. When a sense of trust is established between friends, we then value and respect each other's opinions and only then can we know what to do with a friend's honest appraisal. For instance, if I say to my friend, "The winter colors go best with your skin tones," she won't take my observation as a put-down that she's wearing the wrong colors, but rather as a helpful hint. Or if she should say to me, "I didn't quite understand why you said that to this person," I'll know her words are meant as a mirror in which I can look at myself. My friend's goal is to help me be all I can be.

It's somewhat like my relationship with God. At times things happen in my life that hurt. I could feel betrayed by God, but instead, knowing that He has my best interest in mind, I can thank Him and seek to learn through the hardship.

Even though a friend's words might be hard to hear, I can accept them because a level of trust, love, and respect exists between us, and I know that what motivated her to say these words wasn't her best interest but mine.

A GENTLE REMINDER

I have a friend who I know really loves me, and at times she'll look me in the eye and say, "Coke, you know I love you, and there's something I need to say to you." I know she's going to have a word of correction for me but, as my friend, she's earned the right to be honest. I know she's not out to change me but instead looks out for those things in my life that might stunt my spiritual growth.

—Colleen

Besides a climate of trust and respect, another critical factor in accountability is knowing under what circumstances we should speak the truth in love. How do we know when we should "wound" a friend? What we need to look for is a pattern or trend in a friend's life that holds potential for danger.

Throughout the Scriptures we see that God is very gracious—He looked for patterns in a person's life. For instance, God called Abraham a righteous man even though in Genesis 20 Abraham lied to Abimelech, king of Gerar, saying that Sarah wasn't his wife but his sister. If God always focused on the particulars we'd be in big trouble. Yes, Abraham did lie, but that wasn't a pattern in Abraham's life and therefore God could call him a righteous man. We are responsible for the particulars. When we have sinned, we must confess. But I find great comfort in the fact that God is far more interested in the pattern or the principle than the particular.

He saw Abraham in the context of the bigger picture, and likewise we need to see a friend in the same light. Is what needs to be corrected a pattern? Is your friend making a series of unwise financial decisions? Is she always coming to you with complaints about her marriage rather than confronting her husband? If we focus on the pattern instead of the particular, we will be more likely to overlook the petty annoyances that can bother us about a friend. We will care about the direction a friend's actions may be taking her. Our words should help our friend take a long, hard look at her present actions as well as see where they could lead in the future. When it comes to dealing with a friend's "broad pattern" of behavior, look back on your own experience and don't hesitate to share the things you've learned.

Before you say anything, take a minute and look at your reasons for speaking the truth to a friend. Many times what we have to say is not necessary, simply because the basis of our comment is a petty preference or annoyance. At times when we try to "straighten out a friend," we tend to couch our words in spiritual terms such as, "I'm really trying to help you here," or "You really need to see this side of yourself," when in reality we're motivated by our own interests—by what we'd like them to stop doing or by what we'd like them to be or do.

When we speak the truth in love, we need to make a distinction between conviction and emotion. Maybe a friend is buying a new home, one that you think is too expensive and could strap her financially. Is your counsel against the purchase based on jealousy or on genuine concern for her because you believe she is rushing into the purchase? Is the source of your counsel the knowledge that people who overextend themselves financially often end up destroying their relationships as well as their financial base? If that's the case, then speak out because you're working from a conviction, not an emotion.

When we speak out, we should make certain we aren't doing so to vent our own feelings or as a projection of our own weaknesses. Often what bothers us most in others is what bothers us most in ourselves, and it's those things we're so quick to point out in a friend. In the past, if I'd ever catch myself being critical of my children, I found I had to look deeper to make sure my criticism wasn't simply an extension of something I didn't like in myself.

Choosing Your Words Wisely

The spirit in which we correct a friend is critical. Fortunately, Scripture gives us guidelines. In Galatians 6:1 Paul writes, "Brothers, if someone is caught in a sin, you who are spiritual should restore him gently."

In this verse two words stand out. The first is "restore." In Paul's day the word *restore* was a medical term used to describe how a surgeon would set a fine bone in a hand. I believe Paul specially chose this word as a way of saying to the people in Galatia, "If you want to get involved in holding someone accountable, you'll do well if you use the same delicate care as a surgeon setting a bone."

The second word that stands out in this verse is *gently*. We need to be gentle in how we restore a friend. Gentleness comes when we are attuned to the pain our words might cause another. In other words, the pain we are going to cause our friend should be equal to the pain we'll feel in having to speak the truth. Before I say anything, I will have thought about it, painfully thought about it. I will have prayed about it, painfully prayed about it. I will have sacrificed by spending extra time praying about whether I should say something and how I should say it. I might even choose to go without lunch one day so I could spend that hour in prayer. Saying hard things to a friend should require such care.

Before I say the "hard" thing to a friend, I will make certain I have restocked my shelves with the spiritual resources of love, joy, peace, patience, long-suffering, gentleness, and goodness so they may color and cushion everything I say. As I speak the truth in love, my friend should sense my spirit of love, not my anger or annoyance.

VISIBLE SUPPORT

When a friend of mine began to walk away from the Lord, I gently tried to show her where the decisions she was making might lead. Rather than say, "You're bad, get back in shape," I let her know that I loved her, I was her friend, and I was going to pray for her. My goal wasn't to harp on her but instead support her with my presence and prayers.

—*Stormie*

If I say something and there's no pain involved on my part, I'm going to sound glib. I'm going to say things I shouldn't say. I'm going to be judgmental. I'm going to rush in and walk all over my friend's feelings. But if the pain I feel is equal to the pain I'm going to cause, then I'm not likely to destroy a friend in the process. I'm going to speak with a great deal of thought, concern, and sensitivity.

———— ✺ ————

When we have something hard to say, often we're a little uncomfortable. After all, a certain amount of judgment is involved when we offer counsel and we're suddenly positioning ourselves as "the wise observer." How you say something as much as what you have to say can lessen the feeling of passing judgment on a friend.

For me, I'm most comfortable using questions rather than statements. For the friend buying the new home, rather than saying, "That doesn't seem like a wise idea," you might try helping her explore some of the possible consequences by asking, "What kind of pressure do you think a higher mortgage is going to put on your marriage?" For the friend who shares her frustrations about her marriage with you rather than her husband, you might want to ask, "What are some of the consequences of not talking to your husband about this?" or "What scares you about talking to your husband about this?"

Your questions are not a means to violate your friend's privacy, but rather a way to help her get the wheels of her mind going in a direction they might not have otherwise gone.

Speaking the truth in love takes sensitivity and that too can be conveyed in phrases like, "May I just make an observation," or "May I just ask a question?" Try not to offer immediate solutions, but instead help your friend look for alternatives.

When we carefully choose our words and avoid coming off as judgmental, the hard things can be said and the friendship remain in tact. However, if we're not cautious we run the risk of destroying a person and ruining a relationship that may be salvageable.

Holding a friend accountable is probably one of the toughest challenges of friendship. If the friendship is a true friendship—one based on mutual trust, respect, and love—we should be able to say those hard things and have the friendship survive. When we speak the truth in love to a friend, our ultimate goal is to help her become all she can be.

Make It Happen

1. Think of what you're planning to tell a friend. Now, put yourself in her shoes. How would you want the same information conveyed to you? What words would you like to hear? In what setting would you feel most comfortable hearing "harsh" words? Modify your words and

delivery until you're confident that you'll be delivering them in the softest and most compassionate manner possible.

2. While a friend's need for correction may become suddenly obvious to you, hesitate to offer your friend advice until you've had ample time to think through your insights, check your convictions against Scripture, and seek the Lord's direction. Some of the urgency may fade and you'll probably be better able to express yourself as well as be of greater help to your friend if you give yourself time to think first.

3. What was the most recent gentle admonishment you heard from a friend? Has it been months, even years, since a friend has offered her counsel and advice? If so, then look at your friendships. Are you allowing your friendships to mature to a deep enough level that accountability is possible? If not, then explore why you seem to be building a barrier around yourself.

A Word About Pet Peeves
Kelsey Menehan

Irritations are the black sheep in the family of negative emotions. Better to say we're morally outraged about poverty than to admit that someone's way of eating, talking, or breathing drives us crazy. What's a person to do about those nettlesome irritations? Some of my most cherished friends drive me wacky from time to time. Do I grin and bear it? Tell the person in no uncertain terms to cut it out? Or try to overwhelm their irritating habits with kindness?

To deal with people who rub you the wrong way, you need to realize they irritate *you*, not necessarily anyone else. Sitting at the table with that lip-smacker at the church retreat, I remember being amazed that no one else seemed to notice this offensive behavior. However, most of the things people do that bug us simply reflect different preferences, upbringing, or cultural background.

This perspective certainly helps me deal with my friend Meg, who used to make me seethe inside with her barrage of conversation. Only when I attended her wedding and saw her in the context of her family did I have a new understanding of her conversational style. Only the loudest, most dramatic orator prevailed and Meg could hardly get a word in!

In the realm of close personal relationships you may find yourself becoming *more* irritated with your close friend than with acquaintances or colleagues. However, we're usually more motivated to talk with our close friend about the things that bug us than we are with more casual acquaintances. When our primary goal is building a mutually satisfying relationship, the stakes are higher. But our sense of commitment to the relationship should help us feel safe enough to confront and compromise.

I have a close friend who is a neatnik. Almost before I've finished drinking my lemonade, she swoops down and rushes my dirty glass to the sink for washing. On the other hand, she finds me impossibly scatterbrained. We used to get into silly little tiffs about these foibles. Finally, we decided it wasn't worth it. She'll always be a little compulsive, I'll always have my head a bit in the clouds. But that's okay. We've chosen not to be irritated—at least not all the time.

If we're not careful, people's irritating behaviors can obscure our view of their good qualities. If my friend's compassion seems to carry the same weight as her lip-smacking, perhaps I need to take a second look at what I value in the relationship.

Besides, if nearly everyone seems to irritate me, it's time to take a closer look at my own inner life. Am I angry about something or at someone? Am I under so much stress that little things are getting to me? If I take time to be alone with God, I often discover what is at the root of my prickliness—exhaustion, hurt, bitterness, wanting to be in control. If I give myself a little space and quietness, I can let go of some of those things and allow the peace of Christ to reign again.

—From *Today's Christian Woman* (May/June 1990)

13

Is It Possible to Make Friends With Women of Different Ages?

—Colleen Evans

WHEN WE LIVED in Washington, D.C., a group of young women at our church formed a covenant group and asked me, as well as my dear friend Honni Smith, to join them. We were flattered to be asked and soon became the "older" women in this group. To this day, proudly displayed on my refrigerator, is a picture of a young woman named Wendy and her baby—my special friend from another Washington arena in which Wendy and I worked together for a number or years.

In a sense I became a second mom for Wendy. I saw her through her courtship, her marriage, and the birth of her first child. Wendy seems like extended family to me, and because of our friendship there is a richness in my life I wouldn't have otherwise experienced.

But beyond that, my friendship with Wendy helped me see life through the eyes of a young mother today— a mother who works outside the home to make ends meet because of tough economic times. My friendship with Wendy has prevented me from becoming judgmental of the younger generation. Because I know firsthand what Wendy wrestles with, I'm far less likely to say, "She's not raising her family the way I did it; so she's wrong." I quit work to raise my children, but through my friendship with Wendy, I now understand career mothers much better and no longer am I tempted to be critical of those today who live life differently from how I did at the same age.

We need cross-generational friendships—the benefits are many to both younger and older women. Beyond that, such friendships are represented in the Bible—just look at Ruth and Naomi, or the Titus principle of younger and older women spending time together and learning from one another. As I can attest, cross-generational friendships are enriching and possible, but they are not always that easy to form.

What to Look For

From time to time, I've heard younger women say, "I wish I could find an older woman who understood what I'm dealing with, but that doesn't seem possible. My life is so different from what hers was like at my age." While that might be true, what a younger woman needs to look for in an older woman is not someone she can perfectly identify with in terms of lifestyle, but rather someone whose attitudes she admires. If a younger woman hopes to find an older woman who shares exactly the same circumstances in life as she has, chances are she'll spend a long time looking for that person. Such a match would be very rare indeed.

What should draw women together is not so much the way we live our lives, but rather the attitudes with which we face life. A younger woman should seek out mature women who make her say, "When I get to be that age, I would like to have some of those qualities." Or, "I liked that quality I saw when she reacted to this difficulty or responded to that hurt or loss." Those qualities worth emulating include a generous attitude, a loving spirit, an adaptable disposition, or a grateful heart, to name a few.

Louie's mother, who is now ninety-six, is a very close

friend of mine—we became friends even before Louie and I were married. She is perhaps the most grateful woman I've ever known. It is her attitude of thankfulness that I've wanted to catch from her through the years. She appreciates *everything* God does for her. She will say, "Cokey, I am so filled with joy. God has been so good to me." And then she'll name all the blessings in her life—her health (despite her failing eyesight), her family, her friends, the wonderful place she lives, which happens to be a simple setting. Her focus is on the positive.

When her husband died, we went out to be with her and I thought, *This will surely be a time when she's going to be down.* Instead, she was so grateful that God had allowed her to take care of Louie's father until the day he died. Joy was her predominant emotion. I remember her telling me, "I will miss him. Life will never be the same without him, but do you realize how good God has been? All my married life I prayed that I could take care of Louie's father until the day he died. God let me do that, and I am so filled with gratitude."

GET RICH QUICK

One of the best ways to get rich quick is to find a friend from every age group. If all our friends are the same age, we're destined to become stodgy people and lose out on a wealth of enriching experiences and chances to grow. We each have something to give to women of different ages. Not only is it possible to make friends with women older or younger than ourselves, but it's imperative.

—*Stormie*

Example is a powerful tool. For me, Mother Evans

has been an example of how incredibly healthy it is to have a grateful heart—to appreciate what God has done and to enumerate His blessings. Like the old gospel song, "Count your many blessings. Count them one by one," she does that every day of her life. And because of that, she's wonderful to be around.

Cross-generational friendships help younger women define what is of real value—our attitudes toward life. It also helps younger women realize that though they may be enduring tough times now, with God's help and the right attitudes, they can survive emotionally intact.

Making the First Move

Cross-generational friendships, much like cross-cultural ones, take a bit more cultivating because society doesn't help us with them—we aren't automatically put together. Even within the church we're often separated into groups solely on the basis of age. So for cross-generational friendships to happen we have to seek one another out. We need to be intentional about creating opportunities for such friendships and nourishing those friendships once they happen.

Generally speaking, younger women need to make the first move in establishing contact. Simply put, I think it would be rare for an older woman to feel comfortable saying to a younger woman, "I have some wisdom to share. Would you like to meet together once a week?" Personally, I'd feel pushy and presumptuous to say something like, "You need my advice."

For that reason, it's best if the first move is made by the younger generation, and, while it might sound like impossible advice, it does happen. Just last Sunday, two younger women at our church asked me if I'd like to meet with them. Unfortunately, since Louie and I travel often, I had to be honest and say, "I'd love to meet with you, but I may not be available as much as you'd like." However, once I knew their desire, I was then able to link them up with some other women in the congregation.

While it was gutsy for them to approach me, I found it very heartwarming. I came home from church that morning feeling great. When a younger woman makes that first move, she shouldn't be offended if she is rejected. The right match is out there—she needs to keep seeking with a prayerful heart, confident God will guide her to that godly older woman who will be a good match.

Besides the younger women needing to take the first step, I believe older women must be willing to own up to the fact that they do have wisdom to pass on. Now, I've heard many older women say, "I don't have anything to give," but they cut themselves short. Experience is something that you can only get by living. Most women, if they've endeavored to live fully and richly in the Lord, *do* have something of value to share. And once an older woman is asked for her friendship, she needs to be willing and intentional about that friendship. For instance, one of the young women who approached me at church is a pastor's wife. Since we have much in common, I'm going to make a dedicated effort to spend time with her when I am in town. Even if we can't meet as often as we'd like, we can still make the most of the time we do have. And I need the relationship with a younger sister in Christ.

Once a friendship that steps over traditional boundaries is established, nurturing it can bring about many rewards. One reason I so loved Washington, D.C., was its diversity—it was black and white and brown and yellow—a place unlike so many other areas that are segregated by race. Personally, I want to have friends of other cultures, races, ages, educational and economic backgrounds, and that was especially possible in Washington.

While there, Louie and I shared a ministry with Sam and Vickie Hines, a beautiful Jamaican couple who served a black church in the inner-city. In the process, we became close friends with the Hineses. For a while I was Vickie's "white" friend, and she took a lot of flak in her community for her close relationship with me. But we intentionally worked on our friendship until we realized that we'd passed the barrier of race. No longer was she my "black" friend and I her "white" friend. Rather, we were friends who cared for each other and for each other's family.

The same can happen in cross-generational friendships. You may start out as a young friend to an older woman and vice versa, but after a while the barriers will drop as the friendship matures. We have to go against culture to develop these relationships and nurture them because it's important that we don't get stuck in our own cultural ruts. Jesus calls us to follow Him across cultural lines. When we follow Him, race, age, or economics will not matter. C. S. Lewis wrote, "There will be far more diveristy in heaven than in hell." So let's get ready for heaven by crossing these lines right now!

Becoming the True Body of Christ

In Washington, people were often divided according to their political affiliations. Yet I was always amazed that within the church these barriers could drop. I remember during the Watergate days, soon after we'd arrived in Washington, seeing a man who was being prosecuted sitting on one side of the aisle in our church and across the row was the prosecuting attorney. Despite the differences, these two men could sit together in the same church and worship the same God. But that is possible in Christ because, as it says in Galatians 3:26–28, "You are all [children] of God through faith in Christ Jesus, for all of you who were baptized into Christ have clothed yourselves with Christ. There is neither Jew nor Greek, slave nor free, male nor female, for you are all one in Christ Jesus."

What matters is that we are in Christ. He makes the difference. As we seek out friendships we should be willing and able to cross the lines of age, race, or other differences that often separate us because Christ is the bond—the link—that allows us to cross the bridge to friendships between the generations and between cultures.

A MUTUAL TRUST

I love the example of the inter-generational friendship in the Scriptures of Mary and Elizabeth. Mary was secure enough to go to an older woman—Elizabeth—for reassurance; Elizabeth was secure enough to trust a younger woman to be the mother of her Lord.

—Ruth

I find it sad when churches insist on categorizing and segregating people according to age. The church should help us cross lines, not build up barriers between different groups. Of course, meeting with those our age is helpful to a point—most do want to talk about those things we share in common—but we can become very ingrown if all we talk about is baby problems or how to balance career and family. We need to broaden our friendship base to avoid short-changing ourselves and others in the process.

A dear friend of ours, John Perkins, believes that as the church becomes more and more the body of Christ, it will become less and less homogeneous in the process.

Only when we become more of a mix will we truly be operating like the body of Christ. And that mix includes diversity in age as well. I've been to some churches where everyone seemed under age forty and other churches where I saw nothing but white hair. Sadly, in either case, there was little opportunity for crossing the generations, and I don't think either represented ideally what the body of Christ should be.

I often think of heaven as the great equalizer because, as I've said, in heaven we won't be separated by age or any of the other traditional barriers. And with that perspective, I like to think that what we do on earth today in terms of the friendships we seek with those outside our age group will prepare us for our future. Besides, there are so many forces that tend to separate us from those different from us that I believe as Christians we need to actively work at breaking down those barriers society builds.

———— ⌘ ————

Families are so fragmented by distance these days that younger women often need surrogate aunts, mothers, and grandmothers. And what better place to seek out those relationships than within the church. We need to link with one another—younger women need older women and vice versa. And I am one "older woman" who finds such friendships incredibly enriching!

Our church in Menlo Park is starting a program called "Heart to Heart" with the purpose of linking older and younger women in the congregation together. Our church, like many others, had groups for everyone based on age and it saw the need to move beyond those set groups. When that didn't happen spontaneously among the women, "Heart to Heart" was initiated.

Once we are able to build these friendships, then we'll begin to see the many commonalities all Christian women share—our concerns about how we are growing as wives, mothers, and members of society. Beyond that, we can focus on the greatest commonality of all—our faith in Christ. And together, young and old, we can celebrate Christ and emphasize less and less those externals that separate us.

Make It Happen

1. If you don't have a relationship with an older/ younger woman then begin to take steps to seek such a friendship out. The age difference doesn't have to be that significant—even a forty-year-old woman has a tremendous amount to share with a woman in her early twenties.

2. What attitudes would you like to develop in yourself? Do you have trouble keeping your patience or holding your tongue? Look for mature women who have the qualities you are striving to build into your life. Remember, these qualities may not be outwardly evident in a woman—at first glance, a quiet-spirited and peaceful person may seem shy. Take time to carefully observe someone and you might be surprised at the inner qualities you begin to see.

3. If approaching an older woman seems a scary prospect, then consider bringing a friend along. Simply ask if the older woman would be interested in meeting with you and perhaps with your friend as well. The most important thing is to let your needs be known.

4. Look back on your life and think about what you could share with a woman ten years your junior. If time permits, start a list of what you'd have to offer in terms of advice and wisdom. What do you wish someone had told you when you were ten years younger? Then prepare your heart through prayer, asking the Lord to help you be sensitive to the needs of the younger women. Then, when the time is right for a friendship to develop, you'll be ready.

14

Are Couple Friendships Really Possible?

—Colleen Evans

LOUIE AND I HAVE BEEN blessed with several very close couple friendships over the years—especially the couple friendships we made when we lived in Washington, D.C. But these friendships didn't come about by Louie and me saying, "This year we're going to find a couple to be friends with." Instead, our couple friendships had very serendipitous beginnings.

Having left a cadre of good friends in California, I was lonely after we'd moved to Washington. For months I prayed for new friends. I remember telling the Lord how I'd tried to make new friends but nothing seemed to click. Sure, people were cordial, but Washington was a busy city—people were involved in their careers or family and most didn't seem to have time to develop new friendships. Even in church the connections I made with others never seemed to go beyond a courteous, yet warm, response.

One woman I noticed in church, the wife of a congressman and the leader of the congressional wives' prayer group, seemed to hold the most potential as a future friend. I prayed, "Oh Lord, please . . . I'd love to get to know this woman." Only I added, "But she's so busy. She'll probably not have time for me."

One morning in church, that woman and her husband were sitting behind me. After the service she tapped me on the shoulder and said, "Coke, what do you do every Thursday morning?"

"Nothing," I replied. "That is, nothing that I can't change."

"I have the strongest sense that God wants us to be together," she said.

Tears flooded my eyes. For months I had been praying for a friend and here this woman, whom I wanted so to know, was saying, "Let's get together."

The two of us met regularly on Thursday mornings—the chemistry was there and the friendship was immediate. Over time other women joined us. While the group numbered as high as twelve at times, six of us became the constant core.

Eventually one member of the core group said, "Wouldn't it be fun to get our husbands together?" Many of the husbands had met each other briefly in the past, but none truly knew one another. And so we planned a dinner and the six of us invited our husbands. It was an incredible night—everything clicked and the chemistry between all twelve seemed so natural. There was such laughter and fun that at the end of the evening someone said, "I don't think this should be our last time together." Someone else picked up that thought and suggested a dinner date for the following month and soon we became a couples group. Eventually we agreed among the six couples to get together on a regular basis and the covenant group began.

Never before have we been in a group where everyone clicked! Usually just one couple at a time hits it off, but in this case the twelve of us were together for nearly fifteen years until together we went through the agony of losing one couple in death. Those of us who remain are committed to our covenant friendships until death do us part.

The Rarest of All

Couple friendships are rare mainly because they are more complex. The husbands have to get along with each other, the wives have to get along with each other, and then each husband has to get along with the other husband's wife and vice versa—eight relationships in all!

What typically happens though, is you and your husband are nuts about the wife, yet the two of you can't seem to relate to her husband. Or maybe both of the wives relate wonderfully and so do the husbands, yet between the husbands and wives there is no chemistry.

When the chemistry doesn't exist that doesn't mean something is terribly wrong, but rather the match isn't the best. And while the friendship may begin to take root, chances are it won't be as rewarding or as long-lasting as a friendship where each member of the group clicks.

———— ⌒ ————

As you build a couple friendship look for those relationships where there is some kind of connection in every direction among the couples. The husband appreciates the other man's wife and vice versa. Look for a sense that together you're a team. When you find a relationship where the friendships go in all directions treasure it, go for it, work at it because it's very special.

A GIFT FROM GOD

Couple friendships are not only possible, they are God's gift to marriages. Some of the women I consider my closest friends are the wives of men whom my husband considers as his closest friends. Spending time together as a foursome is not only fulfilling and enriching, but our marriage is better because of it.

—Stormie

Knowing how rare couple friendships are is one reason Louie and I make spending time with our couple friends a top priority. In fact, when we moved from Washington, D.C., back to California last year, one dear couple friend, Honni and Bob Smith, moved out here with us. Together the four of us have worked as a team in California, then Washington, and now we've been led back to California to minister together again. We are committed to nurture and cultivate our relationships even to the point of moving together so we can continue to be close and work in partnership with one another. Friendships mean that much!

Don't be discouraged when couple friendships don't come quickly or easily. Keep in mind they are much more difficult because of the added number of people involved in the relationship. Setting your expectations too high by saying, "We must have a couple friendship," only creates stress. Instead, when the opportunities arise, let a friendship flow. If you're open to couple friendships you will find one—maybe not immediately—but eventually you'll find a couple that's the right mix for you.

Many times it's easier to build a friendship with one person and then add another element—say husbands—to the mix, much like what happened between Mary Jane and me. If you and your friend get along, then watch to see if your husbands click when they come together. Get together for dinner. See how it goes. Dinner in someone's home is one of the best ways to get to know another couple because within a home you have the opportunity for sharing and deep conversations, something that isn't always possible in a larger group setting or at a meal out. The focus of your initial contacts should be getting to know one another better and discovering if the chemistry exists. However, don't force things. If everyone clicks, fine. If not, don't feel guilty.

DON'T FORCE IT

Because you are good friends with another woman is not reason enough for your husbands to become good friends. If the chemistry between husbands is not there, don't try to make it happen. You will end up with four frustrated people. Be content just to enjoy your friend.

—Ruth

Try not to be too hard on yourself or to feel that you've failed if a couple friendship doesn't work out. As I said, it takes time to find these rare and wonderful couple relationships.

———— ∽ ————

We have some couples from our early years we've stayed close to, but mainly our couple friendships have happened in our more mature years. Although I don't have a specific answer as to why that's happened, I do attribute a few factors to it. First, the older you are the more you value friendships and the more willing you are to invest time and energy in them.

A second factor is that earlier in our married life our top priority was our family. We once had friends who had twins and, while we know they valued our couple friendship, for a while they had to "drop out" simply because of the demands of two infants. For a year and a half their primary concern was survival—not building and nurturing a couple friendship. As children grow older and your responsibilities aren't quite as physical or time demanding, you'll find more time for seeking out and cultivating the more complex and rare gift of couple friendship.

Keep an Open Mind

As you seek out potential couple friendships, it helps to be open—don't be too set in your idea of what a couple friendship will be like or with whom it will be. You might be surprised to find a single friend who marries a man that both you and your husband enjoy. Although you never considered your single friend as a potential couple friendship, before you know it that's what it is.

Even if you and your husband have very different friendship styles, don't let that be a barrier to forming couple friendships. In most marriages one spouse, often the wife, is talkative while the husband is quiet. A couple may exist with the exact same mix only in reverse—the husband is the talkative one and the wife is the quiet one. And that match, although it doesn't look like it would work, can make a terrific couple friendship.

The differences in personality and friendship styles can even turn out to be good. Differences are great in a marriage because they cause us to draw one another out, and likewise in a couple friendship the differences between the four people in the relationship can be charming and complementary.

Also, I believe it's good for a quiet man or woman to be drawn into a couple friendship with more talkative people as a way of drawing the quiet ones out. Sometimes as a result, within a couple friendship you see a different side of your spouse, and that in itself can be enriching to the marriage relationship.

As you watch for couple friends, consider people who will bring your quiet husband out. Notice those people he seems more verbal and comfortable with and then seek them out as potential friends. Take notice of those people who draw out a quiet spouse without being threatening; look for those who make your spouse feel valued and accepted.

When Louie and I were first married, years ago, we enriched each other's lives because each of us brought

178

the other in contact with people we'd never had as friends before. Through my involvement in the entertainment world, I brought "show business" friends into Louie's life—very different friends to say the least. He, through his contacts with the Christian world, brought friends, like life-long missionaries, into my circles. Our backgrounds were so different that some of Louie's friends raised their eyebrows and said, "You're going to marry an actress—someone who's been in the motion picture industry?" And I'm sure that some of my friends said, "You're marrying a who? A what? A minister? Are you kidding?" However, bringing together our differences made for a much more interesting mix of friendships for both of us.

While it is helpful to look for friends who share common goals and beliefs, be open to those with different backgrounds and lifestyles. Cross the line—don't look for a couple that's a clone of you two. When a couple is different from you, the result can often be a very rich, fun, and stretching relationship.

When it comes to couple friendships, it's important to realize how difficult they are to find. And remember not to become discouraged in the process of looking for the right couple. When you do discover that special couple, make the friendship a top priority. Couple friendships aren't something we can easily calculate—often they are more serendipitous than intentional. What we need to do is be open—keep looking, watching, and praying that God will guide us to a couple who will become heart friends for life.

Make It Happen

1. Together with your husband, seriously look at the demands and responsibilities the two of you must bal-

ance. Can seeking a couple friendship really be a top priority at this point in your life? If the answer is "no" then release some of your expectations and instead see life as a series of seasons—some more appropriate for certain types of friendships than others.

2. Separately, write down a list of what qualities you would like to see in a couple friendship. What activities would you like to do together? What shared interests are the most important to you? Then, take a few moments to compare your expectations for a couple friendship. Are you on the same wavelength, or are your expectations worlds apart? Trying to reach a mutual consensus on your expectations can greatly help you in your search for that "right couple."

3. Consider either forming or joining a couples group at your church. Realize that the main goal in such a group is to introduce couples to one another—not so much to form deep and rewarding friendships. Within the larger group look for a few couples that seem to have potential. One by one, invite each couple to your home for dinner as a way to get to know them better.

Four of a Kind
Janis Long Harris

Realizing that friendships with other couples can be beneficial to your marriage is one thing. Finding and maintaining those friendships is another. It's been my experience, and the experience of many married people I've talked with, that the road to "couple" friendships is fraught with obstacles. Here are a few suggestions for building and maintaining marriage-enhancing friendships:

Actively seek out friendships. Don't wait for friendships to "happen." Follow the example of Leslie and Peter, who realized that after several moves and a major rift in their church, they didn't have any close friends anymore. "We actually sat down with a notebook and thought about what our options were," recalls Leslie. "We picked about ten couples and invited them over, one by one, over a period of about six months. We served a lot of chicken breasts! It's just a trial and error process—a lot of the couples didn't pan out as friends, but some did."

Seek out friendships with people who share your values and interests. Shared beliefs, whether they relate to religion, child-rearing, or social concerns, can draw people together in friendships as well as marriage. I wasn't surprised when many couples I talked to told me that a lot of their friendships started at church. Just attending church services, however, may not be enough to spark warm friendships. Attending Sunday school class, volunteering on a committee, or joining a small study group can provide a niche within which deep friendships can develop.

Nurture the friendships you already have. Good friendships require care and feeding, so don't take your existing friendships for granted. If your friends haven't contacted you in a while, take the initiative and suggest plans for getting together. Model the kind of friendship you'd like to have in return.

Be sensitive to your mate's friendship needs. Like virtually every other issue in marriage, developing satisfying friendships requires compromise. My husband and I don't always agree about which couples we'd like to get together with or, in some cases, whether we'd like to spend time with friends at all. But we've found that, in the long run, we're both happier when we mutually demonstrate that we care about how the other person feels on the subject.

—From *Today's Christian Woman* (July/August 1990)

EPILOGUE

A LIFELINE
FROM GOD

A WORD TO DESCRIBE friends might easily be "lifeline." As Colleen, Stormie, and Ruth have shared through their many stories, it's apparent that a friend is a special person sent to us by a caring and gracious heavenly Father to help us through tough times, share our joyful moments, and somehow make us feel connected in a world that each day seems to spin a little more out of control. Friends are anchors, they are indeed our lifelines. And while friendship styles, needs, and expectations will differ, three worthwhile truths on friendship come through in the wise advice of the contributors.

First, *friendship takes intentional effort*. Friendships don't just happen. They won't mature unless both parties put forth effort. Effort most often is equated with time—time to remember, time to care, time to be together. And while the biggest argument against friendship today is a lack of time, can we really afford not to make time for friendship? Can we hope to survive on a flimsy network of relationships that are made up of nothing more than mere acquaintances? While it takes time to build and nurture a friendship, our contributors have shown again and again that the dividends are truly worth the time we do invest in a relationship.

Tied closely to the need to put intentional effort into our friendships is the realization *we need to give ourselves a little grace*. We won't always get things perfect. We won't always remember. We may not have a soulmate friendship until late in life. We may go through a

185

series of friends—even have times of "friendship drought." But we need to have faith that God will send special people into our lives when and where we need them. Our part is to keep an open heart to how God is at work in our relationships and to show true friendship when the opportunities arise.

And finally, we need to understand that *friendship is a gift from God*—a precious gift to be handled with the utmost care. Those special people in our lives are not there by accident—they have a reason and a purpose in our lives. With that understanding then, as we unwrap God's gift, we need to continually seek His direction in handling each friendship and each day, dedicating it to the Lord.

American essayist and poet Ralph Waldo Emerson aptly summed up the value of friendship when he said, "We take care of our health, we lay up money, we make our roof tight and our clothing sufficient, but who provides wisely that he shall not be wanting in the best property of all—friends?"

God did not create us to be islands, but instead multi-connected beings who thrive on relationships. We need friendships to survive emotionally, physically, and spiritually. As Colleen, Stormie, and Ruth have shared, friends are indeed a lifeline—a treasure worth seeking and keeping polished once we find it. May this book help you uncover the friendship treasures God has planned for you, keep them in a state of constant upkeep, and above all, create in you a thankful heart toward the Lord who sends a special someone into your life.

Today's Christian Woman is a positive, practical magazine designed for contemporary Christian women of all ages, single or married, who seek to live out biblical values in their homes, workplaces, and communities. With honesty and warmth, *Today's Christian Woman* provides depth, balance, and perspective to the issues that confront women today.

If you would like a subscription to *Today's Christian Woman* send your name and address to:

TODAY'S CHRISTIAN WOMAN
P.O. Box 11618
Des Moines, IA 50340

Subscription rates:
    one year (6 issues) $14.95
    two years (12 issues) $23.60